In the
Days of the Kings

Michael Wilcock

D1421838

CHRISTIAN
FOCUS

For
Edward Thompson
who wanted something like this
and his Mum
who suggested I might write it

ISBN 9781845505080

Published in 2010 by
Christian Focus Publications, Geanies House,
Fearn, Ross-shire, Scotland, IV20 1TW

www.christianfocus.com

Cover design by Alister MacInnes

Printed and bound by
Bell & Bain, Glasgow

Mixed Sources
Product group from well-managed
forests and other controlled sources
www.fsc.org Cert no. TT-COC-002769
© 1996 Forest Stewardship Council

FSC

Contents

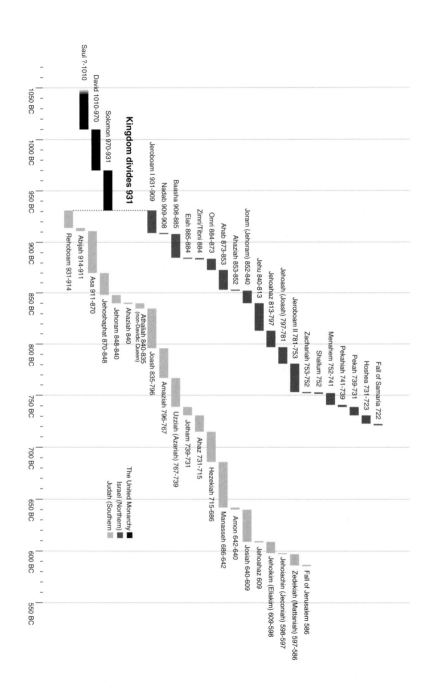

Saul ?-1010
David 1010-970
Solomon 970-931

Kingdom divides 931

Jeroboam I 931-909
Nadab 909-908
Baasha 908-885
Elah 885-884
Zimri/Tibni 884
Omri 884-873
Ahab 873-853
Ahaziah 853-852
Joram (Jehoram) 852-840
Jehu 840-813
Jehoahaz 813-797
Jehoash (Joash) 797-781
Jeroboam II 781-753
Zachariah 753-752
Shallum 752
Menahem 752-741
Pekahiah 741-739
Pekah 739-731
Hoshea 731-723
Fall of Samaria 722

Rehoboam 931-914
Abijah 914-911
Asa 911-870
Jehoshaphat 870-848
Jehoram 848-840
Ahaziah 840
Athaliah 840-835 (non-Davidic Queen)
Joash 835-796
Amaziah 796-767
Uzziah (Azariah) 767-739
Jotham 739-731
Ahaz 731-715
Hezekiah 715-686
Manasseh 686-642
Amon 642-640
Josiah 640-609
Jehoahaz 609
Jehoiakim (Eliakim) 609-598
Jehoiachin (Jeconiah) 598-597
Zedekiah (Mattaniah) 597-586
Fall of Jerusalem 586

The United Monarchy
Israel (Northern)
Judah (Southern)

1050 BC
1000 BC
950 BC
900 BC
850 BC
800 BC
750 BC
700 BC
650 BC
600 BC
550 BC

TO THE READER

With much less of a Christian presence in our Western world than there once was, and very much less Bible knowledge, it is not surprising that many people whom we pass in the street today would scarcely recognize the term 'Old Testament', and that of those who do know what it is many have little idea what is in it. Others, more traditionally educated, may be well aware that it contains colourful characters and strange stories, battles and miracles and kings and things, the patience of Job and the wisdom of Solomon, and Adam and Eve, and David and Goliath, and Noah's Ark, and yet have never worked out how all this fits together and where it belongs in what they think of as 'real history'.

Even those of us who over the years have become familiar with dozens of such Bible people, what they said and did and what happened to them, can find it difficult to carry in our heads what you might call a map of Bible times. By no means all of the Old Testament is a chronicle of historical events, but a lot of it is; and this book sets out to be a narrative of one section of that pre-Christian history, the 450 years during which God's people were not just a nation but also a monarchy. To explain who was who, and who was related to whom; what took place when and where, and how the story connects with that of other nations of the time; in other words, to tell the tale of what happened in and around Israel in the days of the kings – that is the object of the chapters that follow. I have long found these Old Testament characters and their doings both fascinating and challenging, and I hope you will too.

I

THE INVISIBLE KING

What do a provincial capital in western Canada, a state in south-eastern Australia, the greatest lake and the most spectacular waterfall in Africa, and the main railway station of the biggest city in India, have in common?

The Indian city is Mumbai – Bombay, the British called it when they were building its country's railways – and the answer to the question is the name 'Victoria'. In all these places it commemorates the little old lady who at the beginning of the twentieth century ruled from London the largest empire the world has ever seen. Imagine yourself as one of her millions of loyal subjects in those palmy days. As she dies and is followed on the throne by her son Edward, the poet William Watson will write of you all, in his high-flown style, as a people

> *who stretch one hand on Huron's bearded pines,*
> *And one on Kashmir's snowy shoulders lay,*
> *And round the streaming of whose raiment shines*
> *The iris of the Australasian spray.*

Which is one way of saying that a hundred years ago you would have had an idea of kingship (and queenship) rather different from the one that most of us have today. To wear a monarch's crown could mean, and in this case did mean, real power and authority and influence and worldwide fame.

Kings and queens in our day are not like that; and there were others in other periods of history whose monarchies were different again. Not all the rulers of Bible times were rulers of great empires, though some were. Certainly none was what we should call a constitutional monarch. Many, especially in earlier Old Testament days, were of a third kind: they were *little* kings.

Not physically, of course. In fact when the Israelites, migrating northwards after four hundred years in Egypt, first encountered the peoples who lived in and around the land of Canaan, they were impressed by their size: 'So big that we seemed like grasshoppers beside them,' they said. Og, the king of Bashan, was famously tall. Eglon, the king of Moab, was famously fat. And the fortifications of their towns were awesome too. It took a miracle to bring the walls of Jericho tumbling down.

All the same, Jericho was just a town, and we might be surprised to find that it had a king. Even if its territory included the nearby villages and the surrounding countryside it made a very small kingdom. We should be inclined to call the person who ruled such a community a chief rather than a king. In some cases he would have been more like the commander of a garrison. But the Bible uses the language of royalty for kings great and small, and the history of the Israelite kingdoms will gradually unfold the reason for this.

Perhaps we can already begin to see why the boundaries drawn on the maps of Bible lands in those times, about the twelfth century B.C., seem so uncertain. Yahweh, the

God of the Israelites, had promised them the whole land of Canaan, and they did eventually occupy most of it, more or less. Much Canaanite territory they captured and kept. But other areas were not conquered for many years. Still others changed hands more than once, at one time taken by Israel and then at a later time regained by a local king or alliance of kings.

So any map we might try to make would be a patchwork, dominated here by Israelites and there by Canaanites, with shifting, ill-defined boundary lines. And whatever colours we might use for those two nations, we should be needing more. A third one for the Philistines, for example. Their settlements were coastal ones, extending northwards from Egypt about a third of the way up the eastern Mediterranean seaboard. 'Palestine', a useful label for most of the area covered by our map, comes from their name.

They occupied these territories some time after Israel's arrival from Egypt, being part of the big migration of the 'Sea Peoples', as their contemporaries called them, driven from their original homes in the islands and coastlands of the Aegean Sea by political upheavals in the regions we think of as Turkey and Greece. It might seem at first as though their rulers, like those of the Canaanites, were kings of towns. Gath, for instance, was a Philistine town, and it had a king, Achish, who will figure in the story of David. But the Philistines' government was not quite on the Canaanite model. Five of their settlements were each governed by a *seren*, a 'lord', and the nation was ruled by the five 'lords of the Philistines' in a much more unified way than the Canaanites were by their numerous kings. Even so, the frontiers between Philistines and Israelites were not marked by anything like today's border controls. The edges are blurred. We know from the story of Samson in the book of Judges how frequent, and how easy, the coming and going between the two communities could be.

The map would want a fourth colour for the nations to the south-east of Israel. Beyond the River Jordan and the Dead Sea lay the lands of Edom, Moab, and Ammon, three peoples related to the Israelites. Each of these had organized itself into a kingdom which was rather more like a modern nation-state than the others mentioned so far. North of them were the similar kingdoms of the Amorites (not to be confused with the Ammonites; these were unrelated to Israel, and its constant enemies). The gigantic Og was an Amorite king. A fifth colour there, then; and yet another for the Midianites, though they could scarcely be called inhabitants of Palestine. Their home territory was far to the south, but they were mobile semi-nomadic people, who ignored frontiers altogether. In the days of Gideon, raised up to rescue Israel from them, they had joined with like-minded nations from regions away to the east in order to overrun Canaan repeatedly like plagues of locusts, fast-moving camel-mounted hordes intent simply on plunder at harvest time.

They too had their kings. In fact the Israelites were practically the only nation in that place and time which did not. So was Israel what we today might call a republic? Our map would show that the land Yahweh had promised to his people was parcelled out between their tribes, in theory at any rate, in twelve clearly-defined territories, so that perhaps the 'United States of Israel' might be a good name for them. But where was their government? And who presided over it?

The answer had to do with religion, which coloured everyone's life in those days. And for some nations in the ancient world, it was belief in their gods, not the rule of a king, which was the political glue that held them together. A central shrine where the god was worshipped was, as it were, their 'capital', and their daily lives were guided and governed by his priests. That was more or less the case with

Israel, though in some respects the pattern does not quite fit. The Israelites did not have one particular holy place, since their God had had them make a movable shrine to represent his presence among them as they travelled from Egypt to Canaan. At the time we are concerned with, the 'ark of the covenant' (as it was called) happened to be in the little town of Shiloh, but it had several other homes in its long life. The priestly tribe of Levi, too, was not restricted to one place, but dispersed throughout the rest of the tribes.

During Israel's first centuries in Canaan, the guidance of its priests and the laws that God had given it through Moses were all the government it needed in normal times. When a crisis arose, and one or other of the surrounding nations became troublesome, a leader would emerge, a person chosen and equipped by God for the needs of the hour. These were the 'judges' or 'saviours' of Israel. They were not kings; 'in those days there was no king in Israel.'

These words strike one of the keynotes of the book of Judges. They can be taken in more ways than one. By the time they were written, the Israelites had found how good it was to live under the rule of kings who were not only strong and efficient, but also concerned to please God and to care for his people. They might have been forgiven for thinking that the dreadful things that happened all too often in the days of the judges were due simply to the lack of the right sort of government. But they would have been wrong. There were times of peace and prosperity – 'the land had rest for forty years,' 'the land had rest for eighty years,' and the story of Ruth describes life in one such period – when Israel managed quite happily without a king; though the lack of one certainly made it easier for everybody to do 'what was right in his own eyes' (the words that round off the book), and to get away with a great deal of wickedness or folly.

However, to those in Israel at the time who thought it would be a good idea, for whatever reason, to have the sort of king that all the other nations had, a very wise word had been spoken by one of the judges. Gideon was offered the kingship after his great military victories. His response was: 'I will not rule over you, and my son will not rule over you; *the Lord* will rule over you.' True, there was not in the usual sense any king in Israel. But the writer of Judges was not necessarily bewailing the fact, merely stating it. The nation did have a king, and always would have. The alternative to the kind of monarchies that then surrounded God's nation was not a republic. Israel was never a democracy, with 'government of the people, by the people, and for the people.' Like its neighbours, it was a monarchy, but with a ruler far greater than any of theirs: the Lord, Yahweh, was its invisible King.

II

THE 'HOW-NOT-TO-BE' KING

The fourteenth of the judges of Israel was a remarkable man. Among those who had gone before him, you would have to number the years in hundreds, and go right back to the time of Moses and Joshua, to find another such leader. Two books in our Bible bear his name, and it is these – 1 and 2 Samuel – that are the main source for the history not only of Israel's last two judges, but also of its first two kings.

It is possible that each of Israel's tribal territories provided one of the twelve leaders who are named in the book of Judges. If so, it could seem natural that the thirteenth should come from the remaining tribe, Levi, the one that had no territory. Was it right for a member of the priestly tribe to be a political leader? Well, Eli was not a soldier like Gideon, but he could be a judge like Deborah, and as the priest at the national shrine in Shiloh he was well known, and well placed to serve in that way.

And he did so, for forty years. Sadly he is remembered less for the strengths of his judgeship than for the weaknesses that by the end of his life had become only too obvious. His sons Hophni and Phinehas were a pair of greedy unprincipled ruffians who brought the priesthood into contempt, and he totally failed to discipline them. As well as his domestic problems, he had to cope with troubles that began to brew in the wider world. The Philistines had lain low for most of his time in office, but the expansion of their rule was never far from their minds, and towards the end of Eli's ministry Israel found that it was going to have to defend its hard-won western lands by force of arms. An army was raised, and battle was joined at Aphek, twenty miles down towards the sea from Shiloh.

The Israelites were defeated. With an odd mixture of faith and superstition, their leaders reckoned that now their only hope of success was in God, and that therefore it would be a good idea to fetch from Shiloh the sacred 'ark' which represented his presence, and take it with them to their next encounter with the Philistine invaders. If the old priest objected, he was overridden. He was no more able to prevent this folly than he had been able to keep his sons in order.

The result of the second battle was not only another defeat, but also the capture of the ark. It was this unthinkable loss, even more than the loss of Hophni and Phinehas, killed in the conflict, that was the death of the aged Eli too when the news came back to Shiloh. Who now, at this time of crisis for Israel, would Yahweh appoint in his place as its judge and saviour?

The last of the judges was waiting in the wings. Samuel was the longed-for, late-born child of his mother Hannah. At his birth he was so special, and she was so grateful, that she felt this gift from God must be given back to God. Accordingly, she and his father Elkanah dedicated the boy to the service of the holy place at Shiloh, and though visited regularly by his parents he grew up there in the care of Eli, as his protégé and trainee. It seems the family belonged to the tribe of Ephraim, but Samuel became an adopted or honorary Levite, and in due course was even on occasion to act as the nation's chief priest.

But it was as a prophet rather than as a priest that Samuel was going to be remembered. 'The word of the Lord was rare' in the days of Eli, we are told, though a prophetic warning had once been brought to him about his sons' scandalous behaviour. Then came a night when a similar doom-laden message was given to the boy Samuel. 'The priest of Israel slept' (so the hymn puts it), and 'his watch the temple child, the little Levite, kept; and what from Eli's sense was sealed the Lord to Hannah's son revealed.' The prophecy eventually came true with the second battle of Aphek, and the deaths of the old man and his two sons. But long before that, as Hannah's boy had grown his reputation had grown also. To him and through him came the words of God, and 'all Israel from Dan to Beersheba knew that Samuel was established as a prophet of the Lord.' When Eli died, this was his obvious successor.

As for the captured ark, what should have been a triumphal progress through the five cities of the Philistines turned into something quite different. Portents and plagues broke out wherever it came, till panic-stricken Philistia, seeing in these events the fearsome displeasure of Yahweh, sent it back to Israel. There it fetched up not in its previous home (with the priests dead and the ark departed, Shiloh had disappeared from the religious map), but in a new home some way further south, in the town of Kiriath Jearim.

As Samuel's stature increased and his influence spread through the twelve tribes, a change of heart began to stir the nation. The Philistine threat was far from dead, and the Israelites in their anxiety were looking to this new judge for leadership. They were not disappointed. As prophet, he told his people plainly that their only safety lay in a wholehearted turning from sin and to God. As priest, he prayed publicly for them and offered sacrifice on their behalf. And having summoned a nationwide assembly to witness this ceremony, he proved himself to be judge and saviour as well. The Philistines had seen in this gathering at Mizpah an opportunity to destroy all the great and the good in Israel at one fell swoop, and their five lords had quickly mobilized their armies. But Yahweh, controlling the elements as no pagan god could, answered his servant's prayer with a terrific thunderstorm which turned the enemy attack into a rout, and the lords of the Philistines were put well and truly in their place.

But only temporarily. Their garrisons in Israelite territory had not been destroyed; nor had their dreams of expansion. Their continued pressure was one of the causes of the great change that was soon to come about in Israel. Another was the fear that Samuel's sons, a couple of rogues as corrupt as Eli's had been, might succeed him as leader. A third one was the ever-present human desire to be in tune with the spirit of the age, the dislike of being 'different', which is the precise opposite of the distinctiveness, the 'holiness', to which Yahweh repeatedly called his people. The most basic cause of the coming revolution was their lack of the faith which more than anything else should have distinguished them from all other peoples. They may have agreed that the victory at Mizpah had been won because of God's answer to Samuel's prayers, but that, they reckoned, was too chancy a way to run a country on a regular basis. Their kind of believing did not mean actually trusting Yahweh and relying on him in everything.

All these factors came together in the urgent desire for a monarchy. The tide of repentance that had led to that victory had turned completely, to become a tide of unbelief. A deputation representing the whole nation came to Samuel: 'Appoint for us a king to judge us like all the nations.' How insensitive can you be? They saw nothing odd about asking the judge they were rejecting to use his authority to appoint his own replacement. Samuel was deeply hurt, although their rejection of their true king Yahweh was even more serious.

There would be a price to pay, and Samuel spelt it out for them. The cost of a king and a court and a standing army would be ever-increasing taxation, and a central administration whose tentacles would reach out into every area of life. The day would come when they would bitterly regret their choice.

But they were not to be dissuaded. They got their king; though with plans more deeply laid than they could understand, Yahweh saw to it that the person they chose was the one he meant them to choose. A tall, strikingly handsome young man, the son of a wealthy farmer of the tribe of Benjamin, Saul was brought into touch with Samuel, who on Yahweh's instructions first privately anointed him (to his great surprise) as 'prince' over Israel, and then at another big assembly at Mizpah presented him to the nation, which promptly hailed him with the grander title: 'All the people shouted, "Long live the king!"'

'Then Samuel told the people the rights and duties of the kingship'; after which, in something of an anticlimax, everybody went home. If anyone had expected all the trappings of a monarchy to be instantly conjured up, he was disappointed.

The event which confirmed Saul's new status was an assault by the king of Ammon on Jabesh-Gilead, an Israelite town east of the Jordan. Already, just after his first meeting with Samuel, the young king had had an experience of the Spirit of God that had 'turned him into another man'; something similar happened now when the news from Transjordan reached him back on the farm. Like a judge of old, he stood forth then and there as an inspired leader of men, gathering an army from right across the nation and marching out triumphantly to lift the siege of Jabesh-Gilead.

Some years had passed, and Saul was old enough to have a grown son of his own, by the time Israel was again threatened with actual war by Philistia. This son, Jonathan, attacked and destroyed a garrison of the Philistines in his own home territory of Benjamin. It was a spark that ignited major hostilities between the two nations. Expecting reprisals, Saul summoned his troops to Gilgal in the Jordan valley. To their dismay a Philistine army came swarming over the hills in far greater numbers than their own. Samuel had promised that he would come and offer sacrifices to the Lord before Saul's army made a move; but his coming was delayed, and Saul decided to make the offering himself. It was a far-reaching act of folly, not so much because he was the wrong person to offer sacrifices as because he was not prepared to abide by what Samuel, as a prophet of God, had said.

The consequences of Saul's failure to trust and obey were not obvious at once. From this conflict, and from many later ones, he emerged the winner. Besides his Philistine enemies to the west, he had to face the three hostile kingdoms beyond the Jordan (Ammon, Moab, and Edom), the Aramean kingdom of Zobah to the north, and the Amalekites to the south. Against all these 'he did valiantly', we are told.

But his victory over the last-named turned out to be the critical point of his career. Once more a divine word had come to him through Samuel, this time not only promising him the defeat of Amalek but also requiring of him its utter destruction as an incorrigible enemy of Yahweh and his people. So Saul destroyed Amalek – except its king, and the best of its sheep and cattle.

The 'except' sealed his fate. He too was incorrigible.

He would *not* do as he was told. Samuel branded him a presumptuous rebel: 'Don't you see that the Lord is far more concerned with obedience than with offerings and sacrifices? You have rejected the word of the Lord, so the Lord has rejected you from being king.'

The two men were never to see each other again, though Samuel continued to sit as judge in Ramah and Saul continued to rule as king from Gibeah, only a few miles apart – a strange situation! Samuel 'judged Israel all the days of his life', the Bible tells us; while Saul, the rejected, is nonetheless called 'the Lord's anointed' till the day of his death, though his successor had been chosen, and indeed anointed, long since. As Samuel had been ready and waiting to succeed Eli when he died, so David would be ready and waiting when eventually Saul's unhappy and disobedient reign came to an end.

III

THE KING IN WAITING

Another town, another well-to-do farmer, another likely-looking young fellow. Was this the one to replace Saul?

The Lord had sent Samuel on a mission to identify the man he had chosen as the next king. The prophet-judge had travelled south from Ramah, past Saul's base at Gibeah and the Canaanite fortress of Jebus, to the town of Bethlehem. There in the house of Jesse the farmer's sons had been introduced to him one by one. He was greatly impressed by Eliab, the eldest, a big handsome young man, much like Saul in his younger days. But a voice deep inside him said, 'No. Man looks on the outward appearance, but the Lord looks on the heart. This is not the one.' First impressions can be so misleading. Saul was an example of that too.

Not that Samuel's attention was being directed towards someone less good-looking. Looks were simply irrelevant. The right choice turned out to be Jesse's youngest son David, as attractive a lad as anyone could have wished. From the flask of oil Samuel had brought with him, he anointed the boy 'in the presence of his brothers'. Few if any of the people there knew what exactly the anointing was for; all that Samuel had said publicly was that he was in Bethlehem for a religious ceremony. Saul must not yet be alerted to the fact that he had a rival.

Afterwards David went back to the humble job of shepherding his father's flocks on the Bethlehem hills. Sometimes this demanded courage and action, to protect them from predators; sometimes it gave him the leisure to develop his musical gifts. One day he would be famous in both respects, and in the meantime each in turn would be used to bring him to the king's notice.

As had happened with Saul, David had been filled with the Spirit of God when Samuel anointed him. That Spirit, which would have made Saul a great king had he not been determined to go his own way, had now left the older man to his own devices, and a spirit of a different sort often made itself felt. Black moods began to trouble him. At such times he seemed to find some relief in music; and David's abilities in that line were becoming known. The recommendation which brought him to the attention of the king spoke glowingly of many other qualities besides his skill at playing the lyre, but it was for this that he was summoned to the court. Saul took to him at once, and enrolled him on his staff.

'Armour-bearer' was his official appointment, though as from then on he seems to have divided his time between the court at Gibeah and the sheep back at Bethlehem, and as he was not called to accompany Saul on the next major military campaign, perhaps this was just a convenient label. The important thing was that as a kind of therapist he should be on call whenever he was needed.

That next campaign was the occasion that brought David instant fame; and it had nothing to do with his harp-playing. The Philistines were on the move again. The head of the valley of Elah is just over the hills west of Bethlehem, and it runs westwards down to the coastal plain. The invading forces had followed it up into Israelite territory, and Saul had led his troops out to confront them. The two armies had encamped on the high ground to north and south, facing each other across the valley. They were to meet in a battle that would be like no other.

One major change in the way wars were fought in the ancient world had been taking place over the previous two or three hundred years. Bronze, an alloy of copper and tin, was the metal used for tools and weapons in the earliest civilizations, but a better one was discovered in the fourteenth century B.C., and gradually all over the known world the Bronze Age gave way to the Iron Age. Somewhere about 1200 B.C., in the days of Israel's judges, we might date the iron-clad chariots of the Canaanite army that Deborah and Barak had to contend with, and 150 years later Saul found himself hampered by a monopoly on iron-working that the Philistines tried to impose on the people they saw as their subjects.

This change in technology was a gradual one; changes in military tactics could be sudden and unexpected. Aggression from Saul's neighbours might come in many different forms. This time it looked like being a pitched battle, such as he had fought before – until the enemy produced his secret weapon. The Philistine ranks parted, and out stepped Goliath, a terrifying giant of a man, with bronze armour but an iron-tipped spear. (Some of his armour recalls ancient pictures of the heroes of the Trojan War, which may have taken place only a century or so before this.) The proposal was that Israel too should produce a champion, and the battle be decided in single combat. Far less bloodshed, of course, but the consequences would be no less serious: the independence of a nation could be at stake.

Whoever was acting as Saul's armour-bearer, it was not David. He was over at Bethlehem looking after his father's sheep. But three of his brothers were serving in Saul's army, and Jesse sent him to the camp to take provisions and to bring back news. He arrived in time to hear the latest of Goliath's challenges to the Israelites. He was astonished that it went unanswered, and said that if no one else was prepared to take it up, he would be. The bold claim was heard at the highest level, and Saul was equally astonished to find that it came from his young musician. Against his better judgment, he let the lad go out against Goliath unarmed except for a sling, and the famous story reaches its climax: with deadly accuracy and the force of a bullet the sling's stone struck the giant in his unprotected forehead. With their champion dead, the Philistines abandoned both battlefield and camp, and fled, chased by Saul's men to the very gates of Ekron, the nearest of their cities.

To Saul's mind, one-to-one combat with Goliath had seemed so hazardous that he had offered big rewards, including the offer of his daughter's hand in marriage, to anyone who would successfully dare it. That was why he now enquired rather more closely than before into the background and family of the young man who would soon become his son-in-law. But to David's mind there had been nothing hazardous about it. The Philistine had defied Yahweh, the God of Israel, and Yahweh would without question avenge his name and save his people.

What followed for David was a permanent position at Saul's court, a high rank in Saul's army, a deep friendship with Saul's son Jonathan, and the prospect of marrying one of Saul's daughters; but also, thanks to the tactless songs with which people celebrated the victory ('Saul has struck down his thousands, and David his ten thousands'), a jealousy in Saul's heart that replaced his former liking for David, and quickly turned into suspicion, fear, and hate.

More than once when his mind was disturbed he could not hide his feelings, and actually tried to kill the younger man himself. When his head was clear he would dream up more devious ways of getting rid of him. None worked. From situations of extreme danger in which Saul hoped he would perish, David returned covered with glory and more popular than ever. Saul tried to draw his servants, and even his children, into his plots, but came up against a solid wall of loyalty, not to him but to his rival. They all loved David. Everyone did.

In fact Saul's daughter Michal, David's wife, and her brother Jonathan were each able to foil one of their father's murderous schemes. But in the end David had to run for his life. He went first to Ramah, to ask Samuel's counsel; then with a few faithful friends to the town of Nob, apparently a Levite centre as Shiloh had been, where the priests helped him on his way (and would later be put to death for having done so); then, greatly daring, to the Philistines at Gath, Goliath's home town. He hoped they might be friendly, now that Saul was as much his enemy as theirs. They, not surprisingly, saw things differently, and he was soon on the run again.

Before long it was plain to all that Saul would not rest till David was dead. The affairs of government were neglected while he pursued his own private war. No wonder the Bible speaks of the discontent, debt, and distress that drove so many to join David's band of outlaws; though there were plenty of others eager to keep in with Saul by betraying his enemy to him. Some of David's friends thought that he was making things needlessly hard for himself by refusing to harm the Lord's anointed king, though he twice had the opportunity to do so.

In the end he decided to take refuge in Philistine country once more. This time, being now the leader of an efficient fighting force which the Philistines might reckon would side with them against Saul, he was welcomed by the king of Gath, Achish. For war was again in the offing, though still more than a year away. In the meantime David, his soldiers, and their families were allowed to move into the town of Ziklag. From there they went out regularly like a band of brigands on border raids. When Achish asked him where, David would wave a hand airily in the direction of southern Judah; he had in fact been attacking not his fellow-Israelites, but the settlements of their old enemies the Amalekites.

At last the lords of the Philistines were ready for their fiercest assault yet on the neighbouring nation. (Achish found that his four colleagues did not share his confidence in David's pro-Philistine sympathies, and he had to ask him to go home to Ziklag. It was just as well that David's conflicting loyalties were not put to the test.) This time the armies of Philistia marched fifty miles and more up the coast before turning inland, well to the north of most previous campaigns. Saul had seen it coming, this final test of his kingship, and he feared it. He had long chosen to trust his own abilities rather than his God, and now they were all he had left. He tried to pray, but he himself had shut that door, and now it would not open. If only he could ask for Samuel's help, as David had done; but by now Samuel was dead. Perhaps, even so – a séance? a medium? He himself had outlawed such people long before, but he managed to find one, and asked to speak with the prophet's spirit through her.

To her terror, Samuel actually appeared to her, not just a voice but a vision, an august god-like figure wrapped in a prophet's robe. Saul could not see him, but he did hear his words: nothing new, simply that the doom predicted long before was now about to fall upon the disobedient king.

And it did. Battle was joined next day in the valley of Jezreel, and the Israelites were driven back southwards the way they had come, into the Gilboa hills. Saul's sons were killed, even the valiant Jonathan; and Saul himself, badly wounded, fell upon his sword rather than let himself be captured. The reign of the 'how-not-to-be' king was over. The stage was set for his successor, the man who was to be the greatest of all Israel's kings in the days before Christ.

IV

THE GREAT KING

We may reckon the year 1010 B.C. as the one in which David became king. From here on, most such dates can be calculated fairly exactly (the reader will find a note on this at the end of the book); they are much less certain as we work backwards through Saul's time and into the days of the judges, but at least we are right to think of Israel's monarchy first appearing in the eleventh century B.C., as far back before the time of Christ as William the Conqueror and the Battle of Hastings came after it.

So David 'came to the throne'. But if when we read those words we see in our mind's eye the great king of Israel triumphantly enthroned in his palace in his capital city Jerusalem, that picture is altogether too grand and too soon. He did not have a throne, or a palace, and Jerusalem was not even an Israelite town yet, let alone the nation's capital. As at the beginning, we may need to revise our ideas of this 'kingship' that was now David's.

For a start, it had come to him following a battle which his nation had lost, not won. Ironically, it was a Philistine victory that made him king. To begin with, of course, the lords of the Five Cities would not have recognized that title. Look at it from their point of view. They see him as an able leader who has changed sides. Only Achish of Gath has been willing to risk having David's men fight alongside his own on the battlefield, and the other lords have overruled him; but now the battle is over, and while the Philistines do not occupy the whole country they do control it all. They are happy to have David as one of their many vassals, and they are his overlords. For the moment Ziklag is his base; but *king* of Ziklag? Hardly likely.

When David had marched off to war alongside the men of Gath, the pestilential Amalekites, who were a thorn in the flesh to everyone living at the southern end of Canaan, had taken the chance to raid and plunder settlements right across the area. David, sent home from the muster of the Philistine forces, came back to Ziklag sooner than expected. Finding the place devastated, he was able to catch up with the raiders, teach them a sharp lesson, and bring back the loot and the captives they had taken both 'from the land of the Philistines and from the land of Judah.' Great was his popularity among both peoples, especially Judah, his own Israelite tribe. (There seems to have been some redistribution of wealth, to their benefit!)

In spite of Saul's shortcomings, most in Israel were as keen as ever on being ruled by a monarchy. It need not be hereditary, although most of the surrounding kingdoms were, and one of Saul's sons, Eshbaal by name (he is called Ish-bosheth in the books of Samuel), had escaped the carnage at Gilboa and been set up as king in Transjordan. To the people of Judah David was the obvious candidate, whether or not they knew that he was already God's choice, and that Saul himself had accepted the fact long before he died.

So David moved from Ziklag to Hebron, in the centre of

their territory, and was there acclaimed 'king over the house of Judah'. The Philistines had no objection, regarding him as a vassal who would rule Judah on their behalf; so everyone was happy, except Eshbaal and his supporters. They had crowned their man 'king over all Israel'; they had something of a hold on the northern and eastern tribes and reckoned they had a right to the rest.

It suited the Philistines to have Israel split in two. 'Divide and rule' was their motto. They were less pleased when the conflict between the two royal houses, which had dragged on for a couple of years, began to tip definitely in David's favour. Abner, a cousin of Saul's and formerly commander of his army, was the strong man in Eshbaal's camp. He quarrelled with his royal master, changed sides, and went to negotiate with David a reunion of Israel's two halves.

From one point of view it all ended in tears. Joab, the commander of David's forces, had had a brother killed by Abner in a border skirmish, and in revenge murdered Abner as he was leaving Hebron after the peace conference. Eshbaal did not long survive the death of his general; he too was assassinated, by two thugs aiming to curry favour with David.

David for his part was deeply distressed by all this. He grieved for the deaths of Abner and Eshbaal, as he had lamented those of Saul and Jonathan. He had not wanted any of these killings, as he made very clear, and he dealt with the killers at once. But there is no denying that he benefited in consequence of them. In fact consequences followed like a row of falling dominoes.

Because of Abner's murder and Eshbaal's inadequacy, the northern tribes had already been doubting whether it was a good idea to try to carry on independently of the south. When they lost Eshbaal too, and saw David's reaction to these events, and reflected that here was one who combined the glamour of the new monarchy with the gifted leadership of the old judges, their minds were made up. 'All the tribes of Israel came to David at Hebron' and 'anointed David king over Israel'.

The consequence of that was that the Philistines saw a reunited Israel slipping out of their control. Twice their armies drove into the heart of Israelite territory, to reopen the breach between south and north, to 'divide and rule' as before. But twice David's armies drove them back, the second time for good.

The consequence of *that* was that David saw the strategic value of what could have been an ongoing problem: the non-Israelite settlements so long dug in across the centre of the land, Canaanite towns and Philistine garrisons, offering an easy way in for such invaders. There, he decided, he would fix the centre of his kingdom, neither southern nor northern, a place that would be above tribal jealousies. The Canaanite fortress of Jebus would become his capital. The fault line between north and south, the weak point, would become the strongest point, the weld.

The Jebusites believed their little city was impregnable. David proved them wrong. He captured it, enlarged it, and gave it even better defences. He resurrected its old name, Jerusalem, and gave it a new one as well, City of David; 'Davidopolis', we might say. He had a royal palace built for himself, his many wives and children, his staff and ministers of state. Israel had not only freed itself from the Philistines, but now ranked alongside them as a sovereign state. The materials for David's palace, like the site of his city – where did they come from? No tribe of Israel could claim the honour; the latter was contributed by the men of Jebus, the former by the Phoenician king of Tyre. David was no mere tribal leader, but the ruler of a nation, with international standing.

We cannot help noticing how the history of Israel moves forward on two levels. The people of Israel had been wrong to demand that judges should be replaced by kings; as so often, they were dissatisfied with Yahweh's methods of doing things, and thought they knew better. But at the same time, the change was part of Yahweh's plan. He had intended from the start to turn Israel into a monarchy, and would teach his people even more about himself through the kings than he had done through the judges. In a similar way, there is more than meets the eye in David's next grand plan. The books of Chronicles record his proposal to a national assembly: 'Let us bring back the ark of our God.'

At one level, this is simply David wanting to make Jerusalem the religious centre of the country, as well as its political centre. We have seen the ark, the gold-plated box that stood for Yahweh's presence among his people, first in Shiloh, then travelling round Philistia, then returned to Israel and housed for many years at Kiriath-Jearim. Now we are to see it taken to the new capital.

But the Bible is also telling a deeper story. Yahweh was a speaking God, who always directed his people's ways. He gave them messages through prophets like Moses. He had Moses make the ark, where he promised to meet them. He appointed priests to serve at its shrine, and to them he gave a method of casting lots (no one now knows quite how it worked) which gave 'yes', 'no', or 'no reply' as his answers to practical prayers. And from time to time he filled particular individuals with his Spirit, to be inspired leaders of the nation.

All this underlies David's present project. The way the Israelites' God had guided them in the days of the judges came to a climax with Samuel, the last and greatest prophet of that time. Then the Spirit filled Saul when he was anointed king, and David when he was. Saul's inspiration deserted him; turning at the end of his life to prayer as a last resort, he got no answer. But in those dark times David looked to his friend the priest Abiathar, a refugee from the massacre at Nob, and was repeatedly given the clearest 'yes/ no' guidance through him. Now that he is king, he wants to bring his people back to the same way of thinking.

Hence his words to the assembly: 'Let us bring back the ark of our God, for we did not seek it' – that is, enquire at it – 'in the days of Saul.' Meaning of course that Saul did not seek it, or seek God, either for himself or on behalf of his people, until he had put himself beyond earshot of any reply. He did not ask for Yahweh's guidance, still less submit to it. That would be the great difference between his reign and David's.

It was what impressed God's New Testament people when they linked David's story with the events of their own day. In Acts 13 the apostle Paul is reminding a Jewish congregation about its own forebears: 'They asked for a king, and God gave them Saul; then when he had removed him, he raised up David to be their king. Concerning this man he testified, "I have found in David the son of Jesse a man after my own heart, *who will do all my will.*" Of this man's offspring God has brought to Israel a Saviour, Jesus' – one who is like his famous ancestor *particularly in this respect*: one who, as the New Testament says, can claim always to seek not his own will but the will of the God who sent him.

David's obedience was not quite so constant. As Saul never actually repented of his wilfulness, but did occasionally have a fit of remorse, so David really was a man after God's heart, but did occasionally have his lapses, and bad ones too. Unlike his great descendant, he was only human.

V

ONLY HUMAN

So David brought the ark to its final home in Jerusalem. It was an event never to be forgotten. Two whole chapters of 1 Chronicles are given over to describing what happened and who was involved in the great celebration.

In many ways that day was the high point of David's career. The people of Israel had long been a nation, and were now a kingdom. Its twelve tribes were united, not simply around a king of God's choice, but around one who was resolved to find and follow the way in which God wanted him to rule it. The bringing together of the ark of God and the throne of the king at the centre of Israel was a symbol of this resolve. David would have liked in due course to build for the ark a house as grand as his own palace, but Yahweh said no, that was a task not for his reign but for his successor's. Any disappointment he might have felt was swept away when he was told that God intended (in a different sense) to build *him* a house: descendants, a dynasty of kings, a realm and a throne which would last for ever.

In view of such promises, to describe the day the ark arrived as the 'high point' of David's career does not at all mean that from then onwards it was downhill all the way. Far from it. Unfriendly nations soon found that the warrior band David had gathered round him when he was on the run from Saul had become an army second to none: 'the Lord gave victory to David wherever he went.' Others were eager to make friends and form alliances with him. His people's wealth and power increased as his reputation and influence grew; his fame went out into all lands, says the Chronicler, and the Lord brought the fear of him upon all nations.

Israel reckoned itself much blessed to have such a king, and he reckoned himself much blessed to have the splendid household that gathered round him in the palace built for him by his great friend Hiram, the king of Tyre. After the seven years he had ruled Judah from Hebron, he had brought seven wives and their children with him to Jerusalem, and during his thirty-three-year reign over a united Israel he added more to his harem and family.

But here again Israel's history is being told at two levels. The Old Testament nowhere forbids polygamy, it depicts many a good man married to several wives, and it even suggests that such a large family is a sign of God's approval. Yet at the same time it sets forth at the very outset, in Genesis 2, the ideal of marriage that Jesus will return to in the New Testament, one man and one woman uniting as 'one flesh'. It tells any number of stories about the problems that can arise in multiple marriages. And it shows how in the particular matter of relationships with his women and his children David's career did indeed begin to go downhill. What was at one level a mark of God's blessing was at another level the point of David's weakness, and a place of severe discipline.

Israel was at war with Ammon. The war was entering a new phase; the early rains were over, and David was planning a spring offensive against the enemy headquarters at Rabbah-of-the-Ammonites. (This is one of three Middle Eastern cities – Jerusalem, Damascus, and Amman – which are still today, as they were then three thousand years ago, the capitals of nations.) Once David would have led his armies into battle himself, but now he is a great king, and sends them out under the leadership of another. He meanwhile has the leisure to stroll on his palace roof, the monarch of all he surveys. That includes a beautiful woman in a courtyard in the city below, whom he decides he must have. To marry? No, she is already married. As if he did not have enough wives of his own, he has to have someone else's as well.

The story is told in detail in 2 Samuel. He coveted her, stole her from her husband, committed adultery with her, had the husband killed so that she would be free to marry him, and hid the whole disgraceful episode under a web of deception, a thorough-going cover-up: half the Ten Commandments broken in one fell swoop. Not even David, hugely gifted though he was, could keep to the right path unless he constantly and humbly obeyed God's direction. 'The thing that David had done displeased the Lord', and was duly exposed, to his confusion and shame.

But two good things came out of the affair: a psalm, and a son. David, though 'a man after God's own heart', had shown that he was as capable of disobeying him as Saul was. The difference between them was that David was willing to repent. With his gifts of music and poetry he expressed his repentance in one of the greatest of the psalms, the fifty-first: 'Create in me a clean heart, O God, and renew a right spirit within me.'

The son was not the one born of his adultery with Bathsheba. That child died, the death that its father deserved to die. But to show that the sin was forgiven, God gave them another son. They called him Jedidiah, 'beloved of the Lord'; but he has gone down in history by his other name, Solomon. As with David's own generation, a whole procession of elder brothers would be passed over for this one to become in due course a great king in Israel.

For the idea that the king should naturally be succeeded by his eldest son was by no means taken for granted. The monarchy was far too new; such precedents as there were within Israel pointed in a different direction. Jonathan for example had readily accepted that David, not he, would be king after Saul. The throne was not going to pass to Amnon, David's eldest, either. The only thing that has so far disfigured the portrait of David, his lust for an unavailable woman, is the one thing the records tell about Amnon. It had led David into adultery, and it led Amnon into incest: he raped his half-sister Tamar.

This crime highlighted another flaw in David, and lit the fuse for the greatest crisis of his reign. For all his toughness, he was not good at keeping his family in order. Though very angry with Amnon, he did nothing whatever to discipline him. Enter at this point Absalom, Tamar's full brother: they were both the children of David's Aramean wife Maacah. He was as angry as David was about what had happened, but unlike him was determined that Amnon should not go unpunished. For two years, all unsuspected, he plotted revenge on Tamar's behalf, and when the time was ripe he had his brother murdered. He guessed rightly that David would not do anything about this either, but just in case, he put himself out of reach for the time being by going off to the Arameans at Geshur, from whose royal family his mother had come.

Sure enough he had no need to fear punishment at David's hands. In fact three years later he was back, not as a murderer brought at last to justice, but as a wandering son brought home; though he was still not formally reconciled to his father for two years more.

What began to unfold then was a scheme which may have been in his thoughts, in embryo, even before the rape of Tamar. If the throne were, after all, to go to the eldest son, it seems that with Amnon dead Absalom was next in line for it. Although he was good at nursing grievances over long periods, he had no mind to wait till it came to him by inheritance. He set in motion his plans for a *coup d'état*. He was handsome, popular, clever and unscrupulous, a master of spin and empty promises. He was able to keep David and his advisers totally in the dark as to his intentions, his ever-increasing support among the people, and the forces ready to rally to his cause, until the fateful day when the news reached David that his son had been proclaimed king at Hebron.

Suddenly the true king's eyes were opened to his extreme danger. The community of priests in Jerusalem was loyal to him, and so was the core of his army, the 'mighty men' who had fought for him ever since his fugitive days, especially his 'foreign legion' from Crete and Philistia, the Cherethites and Pelethites. But who else? – for as the Bible puts it, Absalom had stolen the hearts of Israel.

David knew however that he could find friends and supplies beyond the Jordan, and the road down eastwards from Jerusalem was really the only possible escape route. He was a fugitive once more. He and his company got away just in time, and reached the river as Absalom's forces entered the city.

Had the younger man followed up his advantage immediately, the kingdom would have been his for the taking. But his inexperience, together with misleading counsel from an adviser planted by David, made him delay in order to muster a larger army, while his father was given a breathing space to cross the river, find help and reinforcements among his Transjordan friends, rally his troops, and choose his ground for the battle that ensued.

Experience told. The rebel army was defeated, Absalom killed, and David restored to his throne. But Israel could not go on as if nothing had happened. Rivalries between the tribes had come to the surface again, and rivalries between military commanders. People found fault with David for his extravagant grief over the death of the good-for-nothing son who had so nearly destroyed him and had torn the nation apart in the process.

There was to be one more threat to the peace and stability of the kingdom, towards the end of David's reign. Adonijah, we are told, 'was boasting that he was to be king'. Another son from David's Hebron years, with much support in Judah and the south, next eldest after Absalom, with powerful friends in high places, and to cap it all a very handsome man (like Absalom, and like Saul) – he seemed to have everything going for him. These however were the very facts that suggested to people of insight that he was precisely not the man Yahweh would choose to rule the united tribes of Israel.

At an *al fresco* dinner party by the spring of En Rogel just outside Jerusalem, Adonijah was announcing to his eminent guests that he had now succeeded David. But the old man, though feeble, was not yet dead. The royal edict went out to the group of even more eminent people gathered round his bed that Solomon, not Adonijah, was to be the next king. Even as one company was toasting Adonijah, it heard another one cheering and shouting half a mile away up the valley: 'Long live King Solomon!'

Adonijah's party broke up in disarray. It had in effect been a conspiracy, and its host and his highest ranking guests would all later pay the penalty. But its result had been to bring the man of Yahweh's choice to the throne while his father was still alive. The overlap, technically known as a 'co-regency', helped greatly to smooth the transfer of power, and was often to be repeated in Israel's later history.

It enabled David, who rallied strongly in his last days, to call a national assembly, described in the closing chapters of 1 Chronicles, at which 'they made Solomon the son of David king the second time'. And when finally the great king 'died at a good age, full of days, riches, and honour', no doubt a third ceremony followed, to acclaim Solomon as sole king; not perhaps greater than his father, but certainly embarking on a reign to be bracketed with David's as the two halves of Israel's golden age.

VI

THE WISDOM AND THE GLORY

The son was to become as famous as the father. A thousand years later, everyone who heard Jesus speak of 'Solomon in all his glory', or of the Queen of Sheba who 'came from the ends of the earth to hear the wisdom of Solomon', would have known instantly what he was talking about. The Bible's account of that state visit shows how Solomon enjoyed international fame even in his own day.

It was the two things referred to by Jesus – the wisdom the queen had heard about in her own country, and the wealth whose glory dazzled her when she came to Solomon's country and saw it – that (as 1 Kings 10 tells us) took her breath away. They sum up the greatness of this third king of Israel.

The wisdom came first. Before David died, he could see something of it in this son of his. There were loose ends that would need tying up after he was gone, in respect of the people involved in Adonijah's scheming, for instance, and others who might threaten the unity of the kingdom. 'You are a man of wisdom,' said he; 'you will know what to do.' Solomon did know, and marked the start of his reign by doing it. One way or another all the possible trouble-makers were dealt with.

There was more to come. He had a dream, in which he was told to ask for whatever he wanted God to give him. Keenly aware of his responsibility as ruler of the people of Yahweh, he asked for wisdom to do the job well. That was itself the wisest request he could have made! The gift was given, and began to show itself in all sorts of ways.

The record begins with his presiding over a court case, and handing down a judgment so keen and so right that everyone was astonished. Then when he turned his mind from law to government, from justice for individuals to the administration of a whole nation, he proved to be equally good at that. Israel was never organized more efficiently than it was by Solomon's civil service.

Of one kind of wisdom there is no mention. Unlike his father, Solomon never needed to know how to fight a war. His long reign, from 970 to 931, was a time of peace; *shalom* is the Hebrew word – it echoes his name. Land-hungry migrants like the Sea Peoples were no longer a threat to Israel and its neighbours, and power-hungry empires in Egypt and Assyria had not yet arisen. David's victories had put an end to warfare within Palestine, and all its kingdoms were either his subjects or his allies. If there was an empire anywhere in the Bible lands of the tenth century, it was the one Solomon inherited.

The wisdom he showed in the governing of Israel can be seen in his dealings with other nations also, both within and beyond the boundaries of his empire. Hiram of Tyre had been a good friend of David's, and his friendship continued in the reign of David's son, though with a difference: these two kings treated each other as equals, but it was Solomon who in their trade agreements contrived to have things his way. Outside the ring of satellite states, other nations too became partners in his enterprises. The fact was that Israel sat astride many of the great commercial routes of the Middle East. Through Solomon's territories goods travelled by land between Egypt and Arabia to the south and Mesopotamia and Asia Minor to the north, and by sea out across the Mediterranean in one direction and down towards the Indian Ocean in the other. There were big profits to be made out of all this international trade, and Israel, and Israel's king in particular, grew rich.

A great deal of Solomon's wealth was pumped into two major projects. Although he never had to go to war, he was wise enough to be prepared for one. He built up a large, well-equipped army, horses and chariots like those of the Egyptians in the days of Moses or of the Canaanites in the days of the judges, and fortified a number of towns across the land as strategic bases for it.

The other project, the chief glory of his reign, was the building of the magnificent temple of Yahweh in Jerusalem. People call it Solomon's temple because he carried the scheme through, but the idea had been David's, and the pattern went back to the days of Moses. Everything you would have found in the tabernacle, the sacred tent that was set up in the Israelites' camp when they were travelling from Egypt, was here in this new sanctuary. Some items, including the gold-plated ark of the covenant, were still the old originals, while many were reconstructions on the grand scale.

So the ark, the symbol of God's presence among his people, was housed at last in a building specially designed for it. This new kind of home itself had a symbolic meaning. For Solomon was a man of peace in more ways than one. Of course peace in the most obvious sense meant no war. *Shalom* meant something better than that – prosperity and well-being instead of hardship and suffering. (Hitler's downfall in 1945 brought 'peace' to Europe, but *shalom* took longer to achieve.) Concerning Solomon's reign, though, the Bible also uses the word 'rest'. It had taken the Israelites forty years to travel from Egypt to Canaan, and many times forty before the turmoils of the move were over and they had really settled down in their new land. While they had lived in tents, God had had them make a tent for him too. Now that they lived in houses, they were to make him a house. Both when the nation was on the move and when it came to rest, it was being shown Yahweh as the God who lived among his people. No wonder that in New Testament times, when the 'place' where God made himself known was actually a person, Jesus of Nazareth, that person would himself be called (as we are told early in John's gospel) both Tabernacle and Temple, God's tent and God's house. No wonder, too, that in 2 Corinthians 5 Paul would describe the mortal body with which a believer travels through this world as a tent, and the one that will replace it when he reaches home in the next world as a house; the first temporary, the second permanent.

If the high point of David's reign was his bringing of the ark to Jerusalem, the same might be said of Solomon's dedication ceremony for the house he built for it. However, it might also be said that the wisdom, if not the glory, of this wisest of kings was already in decline. Was he wise to spend twice as much time on the building of his own house, and vast amounts of money on the defence of his realm? Was he wise to set up a system of forced labour, or to marry into the royal family of Egypt, Israel's historic enemy?

He could have justified all these doings, and the Bible writers do not explicitly find fault with any of them. In fact they speak warmly of the wisdom that God did indeed give him, that everyone admired, and that lay behind practically everything he did during the greater part of his reign. But the first book of Kings does recognize that he was unwise in his relations with women. It was not so much that his wives were many, or even that they were foreign, but that they brought with them the worship of their foreign gods. His great-great-grandmother Ruth was a Moabite woman, but she had renounced the gods of Moab when she married into the Israelite community. In contrast, heathen religion was now not only tolerated but even encouraged in the royal harem, and 'when Solomon was old his wives turned away his heart after other gods.' David had broken a whole bunch of the Ten Commandments in his affair with the woman who became Solomon's mother. It was only one of them that David's son was in danger of breaking, but that was the very first one, 'You shall have no other gods besides me'; and somehow at that crucial point his celebrated clear judgment was clouded.

Because of this his reign was not in the end as peaceful as it might have been. There was trouble in Edom in the south and in Aram in the north, threatening two of the empire's main trade routes. Both nations had been defeated in David's military campaigns and both recognized Solomon's supremacy, but an Edomite prince, Hadad, had returned from exile in Egypt, and an Aramean 'strong man', Rezon, had staged a coup in Damascus, and neither was friendly to the central government in Jerusalem. Hadad and Rezon had been around long before Solomon began to find them a real nuisance; but Yahweh, who knew the end from the beginning, had them ready to be brought into play when in his later years Solomon would need to be taught a sharp lesson.

Head and shoulders above these two mischief-makers stands the figure of Jeroboam. Unlike them, he was an Israelite, in fact a high-ranking official in Solomon's government, very able, and a born leader and organizer: the most dangerous man in the kingdom. His responsibilities were among the northern tribes, as were his roots. As things would turn out, that was also where his loyalties lay, rather than with the twelve-tribe Israel over whose unity David and Solomon (both southerners, of course; that rankled with Jeroboam) had laboured so long.

He was not the kind of man who would care much about a message from Yahweh, but he was willing enough to listen to one that foretold a glittering future for him – nothing less than the throne of a northern Israelite kingdom. It had come to him privately and personally through the prophet Ahijah, but somehow Solomon got wind of it, or at any rate of some suspicious activity on Jeroboam's part. Jeroboam found himself a hunted man, and not being minded to be a martyr to a cause that had not yet even got off the ground, he prudently made his escape to Egypt, like Hadad forty years earlier. There he would bide his time till the death of Solomon, when, as the prophecy itself had said, he might expect it to come true.

In the closing years of Solomon's reign, then, the king was not quite as wise and the kingdom not quite as glorious as they had once been. All the same, it was the wisdom and the glory that would be remembered. He had been an extraordinarily gifted man, as knowledgeable about the world of nature as about the worlds of politics and commerce, famed throughout the nations for just government and shrewd counsel, the ruler of a prosperous and happy people, a great builder, a patron of literature and the arts, and himself a prolific author of the kind of writing that figures in our Bible as the books of Psalms and Proverbs. As the centuries passed, and increasingly as the kingdom declined and finally perished, it was Solomon's reign, together with that of his father David, that Israel looked back to as its golden age, the kind of kingdom that it hoped and dreamed might one day come again.

The Northern Kingdom of Israel

The Southern Kingdom of Judah

VII

NORTH AND SOUTH

It was more than seventy years since 'all Israel' had recognized David as the nation's king and Jerusalem as its capital. Now David's son Solomon was dead, and Solomon's son Rehoboam was to be king. The twelve tribes might not always see eye to eye, but Israel was nevertheless one nation. Its unity had been as real and as important for Samuel, the last of the judges, as it had been for Moses and Joshua when they first brought God's people from Egypt to Canaan centuries before. Then in the early days of the monarchy, Rehoboam's grandfather and father had worked hard to strengthen the one-nation idea, and now he was on his way from Jerusalem to Shechem, the place where Joshua had once convened an historic national assembly, to be acclaimed in his turn as king of 'all Israel'. Who would have believed that within a matter of days the magnificent and united kingdom bequeathed by Solomon to his son would fall apart, never to be reunited?

Just two people, probably. One was Ahijah the prophet, who had been given a message from Yahweh about a cloak torn in twelve pieces. The other was Jeroboam, now returned from Egypt. It was to him that the message had been directed; to him Ahijah had handed ten of the pieces of cloth, and spelled out the meaning of the prophecy. It is unlikely that anyone else foresaw such a tearing apart of the tribes.

The assembly at Shechem had grievances to air, and wanted some assurances from the new king before they would recognize his claims. If, as some think, the 'Israel' gathered there was the northern tribes only (the word 'Israel', already sometimes used in that way, would become their regular name when in due course they became a separate kingdom), and if their complaints about Solomon's harsh policies were justified, then they were expecting either to have the new king accept their demands or to replace him by a northerner. In fact 'all Israel' is more likely to mean the whole nation, and there is some doubt as to whether there were good grounds for their grievances. Either way, the outcome was not quite what most people anticipated.

For when Rehoboam answered the assembly's spokesmen not in a diplomatic, statesmanlike way, but with blustering and threats, demonstrating as he did so that he had inherited none of his father's wisdom, 1 Kings 12 tells us that 'all Israel' rejected him, 'all Israel' stoned one of his chief ministers to death, and 'all Israel' offered the throne to Jeroboam instead – and, to make things plainer still, says that Jeroboam did in fact become king over 'all Israel'. In other words, what the nation thought it was doing was replacing one royal house by another, just as eighty years before the House of Saul had been replaced by the House of David.

But that was not what Yahweh had in mind. Rehoboam was not to be a king without a throne. Israel as a whole might have rejected this foolish man, but his own tribe of Judah, together with its neighbour Benjamin, remained loyal.

There were to be two kingdoms. One would be labelled with the name Israel, but prove repeatedly unworthy of it. The other, though only a fraction of the whole, and often just as unworthy, would continue to have David's descendants as its kings, David's city as its capital, and the promises of David's God to rely on. It was as Ahijah had prophesied, and 'this was a turn of affairs brought about by the Lord'; and when Rehoboam mobilized an army to recapture northern Israel from his rival, Yahweh sent another prophet, Shemaiah, to stop him: 'This thing is from me.'

So the kingdom was divided, and Jeroboam was master of ten twelfths of it. From his point of view, it was a shame that Jerusalem was not included, and he knew that that would cause him problems. One of them was easy to deal with: the northern tribes needed a new capital. Shechem, the obvious choice, was duly fortified and became their seat of government.

Another problem was much more far-reaching, and Jeroboam's answer to it would in the end bring about the downfall of the northern kingdom. When Ahijah had reminded him that Jerusalem was the city where Yahweh had 'put his name', it meant that after the twelve tribes had been torn apart the Davidic kings would still have not only a throne but also a temple – *the* Temple, which was the heart of the faith of Israel. And whatever political boundaries might be drawn across the map, they would not be frontiers in the modern sense of the word, and could be crossed without hindrance. Israelites from both north and south would continue to travel to and from Jerusalem regularly to worship Yahweh in his chosen home. That, the new king told himself, would never do. Rehoboam might perhaps learn wisdom; the attractions of being independent of the House of David might fade; the north might get tired of the House of Jeroboam, abandon the adventure, and reunite the kingdom.

Jeroboam decided therefore that his tribes should have not only a king but also a temple of their own – two temples, in fact, conveniently placed at either end of their territories, one in Bethel and the other in Dan. As well as its own holy places, he would give his kingdom all that went with them, priests and altars and festivals; the package would look like the kind of religion that Israel was used to. But everything would be according to his plan, not Yahweh's. Designed for people who were more interested in the outward trappings of worship than in the God they were supposed to be worshipping, the whole system was a shameless imitation of the one based in Jerusalem, and showed a total disrespect for the historic faith of the nation.

It certainly sorted out the sheep from the goats. Northerners who saw it for what it was, a rebellion against Yahweh, moved down to Judah, and strengthened Rehoboam's cause. As these objectors to the new religious policy ebbed away, Jeroboam too found his grip on his kingdom strengthened. It was success of a kind. But as king after king followed his example, it led to his being repeatedly named by the Bible historians as the one who 'drove Israel from following the Lord and made them commit great sin'; until after two hundred years of such sinning the Lord's patience would finally run out, and he would 'remove Israel out of his sight', sending the northern tribes into exile and captivity.

It was not as if Jeroboam was kept in the dark about the long-term consequences of what he was doing. Yes, he was Yahweh's choice to be the first to rule the northern kingdom, but it was his responsibility to do so in Yahweh's way, and he was left in no doubt that that was not happening. Twice he was confronted by prophets who told him so, and punched home their messages with frightening signs of God's displeasure. But what he heard and saw had no lasting effect, and for twenty-two years he led his people steadily on down the first gradual slope towards ruin.

For three of those years the southern kingdom looked very different. So many right-thinking people had moved down from the north, disgusted by Jeroboam's doings, that the true faith of Israel was flourishing in Judah. What we are told about Rehoboam at this stage is the kind of thing that for the Bible writers indicates Yahweh's approval. He does after all begin to show signs of the wisdom that had been given to his father in earlier days. He marries several wives, and none is a pagan foreigner, indeed all are from within his own clan. He sets about a big building programme, fortifying strategic towns around his kingdom, and gives his sons responsible positions in them. One of these young men, Abijah, he grooms to be his successor.

Yet for some reason in the fourth year of his reign the relationship with his God turned sour. Both king and kingdom seemed to tire of it; so although there was still much that was good in Judah, in the fifth year Yahweh took drastic action to bring them back into line.

Egypt was the means by which he did it. Over the centuries, that ancient nation had seen no fewer than twenty-one royal families come and go, the last being the friendly but feeble one into which Solomon had married. The Twenty-second Dynasty was different. Its first king, the Libyan prince Shishak, was a strong man. Making his presence felt in all directions, he marched his armies over much of the empire David had built up, and captured many of the newly fortified towns in Judah.

A prophet appeared – it was going to happen regularly in both kingdoms – to remind Rehoboam and his people of what they should have remembered anyway: that disobeying God was bound to lead to trouble sooner or later. The prophet was Shemaiah, whom we have met already, and his words were heeded. Judah repented of its sin, and Shishak stopped short of destroying Jerusalem, contenting himself with carrying off vast amounts of the treasure Solomon had amassed there. (This included the hundreds of golden ceremonial shields with which his palace was adorned. Rehoboam put up replacements made of bronze. They looked nearly the same. If you had a short memory, or short sight, you might not notice that things were more down-market than they used to be.)

Once the threat was past, Judah's enthusiasm for Yahweh cooled again. For the rest of Rehoboam's reign the general verdict on the king was that he 'did evil in the sight of the Lord', and the general experience of the kingdom was that it was embroiled in repeated border skirmishes with its northern neighbour. Few people seemed to see the connection between the two.

After Rehoboam's death the story of Abijah's three years on the throne was, by and large, more of the same, but with one remarkable exception. There came a day when hostilities between the two kingdoms flared into a major confrontation, with both kings leading their armies out to war. Jeroboam still ruled the north, and found himself listening to an eve-of-battle harangue from Abijah, addressed not to his own troops but to the enemy. Through this unlikely mouthpiece the army of the north was being told a few home truths. Abijah had grasped a great fact: it was to the House of David that Yahweh had promised his long-term blessing, failures though many of its kings might be (he himself was one such); the House of Jeroboam had only its own abilities to rely on. If the northerners knew what was good for them, they would abandon their king and reunite with the south.

Jeroboam, whose army was considerably bigger than Abijah's, took no notice. He sent a large part of it unobserved round to the rear of the southern troops, and was poised for victory, when Abijah, finding himself surrounded, cried out to Yahweh for help. For that time, at any rate, the beliefs about which he had just been making a speech were real enough for him to put them to the test. His God did not let him down. He won the battle, a slice of northern territory (including the religious centre at Bethel) was captured by Judah, and Jeroboam lay low for the rest of Abijah's short reign.

The next one, by contrast, would be among the longest in Judah's history, and the first that would look something like that of a true, godly, David-and-Solomon kind of king.

VIII

'A SHOW OF EIGHT KINGS'

At one of the more spooky moments of Shakespeare's 'Scottish play', the three witches who cross Macbeth's path from time to time conjure up for him a vision of those who will rule Scotland after him. 'A show of Eight Kings' is what the stage direction calls for.

That is what we see in the two Hebrew monarchies as we look on beyond the death of Abijah. Between the years 911 and 870, while his son reigned in Judah, no fewer than eight men in succession ruled the northern kingdom. Or, if you will, you may discount Tibni, whose claim to the crown was backed by only half the people and none of the army; then you will reckon seven who actually reigned in the north, and over against them the one who in contrast ruled the south for the whole of that forty-one-year period.

Jeroboam and Nadab, Baasha and Elah, Zimri and Tibni, Omri and Ahab – the names, mostly unfamiliar, scarcely make one's spine tingle like Macbeth's nameless apparitions. On the other hand, the prospect of eight kings in four decades promises a story of some excitement; and so it proves to be.

Jeroboam we remember as a man of huge ability and driving ambition. It was with the powerful Egyptian pharaoh Shishak that he had taken refuge in the last days of Solomon, and no doubt he saw himself, like Shishak, as the founder of a dynasty. At any rate there was no question of his not being succeeded by his son Nadab when he died, just a year after Asa had succeeded Abijah in Jerusalem.

Nadab had no thought of making any changes in the way Jeroboam had ruled. 'He did what was evil in the sight of the Lord,' says 1 Kings (which with its sequel is our source for practically all the history of the northern kingdom), 'and walked in the way of his father, and in his sin which he caused Israel to sin.' Unlike the promises Yahweh had made to the House of David, which were unconditional, those he had made to the House of Jeroboam depended on its kings obeying him. This was precisely what they became notorious for not doing. Little wonder then that Nadab's reign lasted only two years. Even now, with the days of Saul and David (not to mention Samson) long past, there was friction every so often between Israel and Philistia. In the course of yet another Philistine war and the prolonged siege of the Philistine town of Gibbethon, and perhaps under cover of them, Nadab was assassinated by one of his own officers. This man, Baasha, took the crown and murdered every possible claimant to it, in fact the entire royal family. Jeroboam, disobedient but (in his own estimation) successful, had ignored the last message brought to him from the aged prophet Ahijah, and this was the doom that Ahijah had then foretold. No dynasty after all, and no legacy but the reputation of one who richly deserved the scathing condemnation Jesus would one day utter: 'Woe to those who sin by making others sin.'

Baasha might have based his claim to the throne on an

older principle than that of hereditary monarchy. In the days of the judges, you emerged at the top by your own gifts and the strength of your personality (or so it probably seemed to people like him, who had not a glimmering of how Yahweh actually worked). So he took over the top job in Israel and held it for twenty-four years, making his capital the beautiful hill town of Tirzah, where Jeroboam had had a royal residence. About halfway through his reign he crossed swords with Asa, as we shall see.

He may have had no hesitation about overriding Nadab's right to inherit the throne, but he seems to have assumed all the same that he himself would be succeeded by his son Elah. Alas, in that respect the House of Baasha would get no further than the House of Jeroboam had done. Elah's reign would last no longer than Nadab's, and he too would be murdered by one of his army officers. Baasha and Elah could not plead ignorance that such a fate awaited their house; like so many others of the northern kings, they had had explicit warnings from one of Yahweh's prophets, in this case Jehu Ben-Hanani, and had taken no notice.

Zimri held the southern command of the army's chariots, based in Tirzah (the northern command was up at Megiddo, a base for such forces since Solomon's time). He plotted against Elah, and surprised him in the middle of a drunken orgy in the palace there. Killing not only the king but also his family and even all who were known to be his friends, Zimri began a glorious reign that lasted all of seven days.

The Israelite army was down in the south-western corner of the country, where Israel touched Judah and Philistia, yet again besieging Gibbethon. It was the kind of campaign in which of course Zimri's chariots were not needed. When the news of his coup reached them, the unanimous cry of the troops was for their commander-in-chief, Omri, to be king, and not Zimri. The entire army marched back to the capital. In contrast to the other siege, which had been in progress, on and off, for twenty-five years, this one lasted less than a week. Tirzah's defences were easily breached, and 'when Zimri saw that the city was taken, he went into the citadel and set it on fire around him, and so died.'

Unlike Zimri's, Omri's really was going to be a glorious reign. So at any rate most of the ancient records describe it; in his time he was famous far and wide. The author of 1 Kings looks at it in a different way. He is not interested in Omri's achievements; he merely notes a handful of facts. This very able man had first to fight for his throne. The army supported him, but half the nation wanted another man, Tibni, as king, and it took four or five years for Omri to eliminate this rival. He built a new capital, Samaria, to replace Tirzah. His principles were those of 'Jeroboam the son of Nebat, and the sins that he caused Israel to sin'. In fact in his twelve years on the throne he 'did more evil than all who were before him'.

And after him, 'in the thirty-eighth year of Asa king of Judah, Ahab the son of Omri began to reign over Israel'. That however is another story. Shakespeare's eighth ghostly king carried a glass through which Macbeth could look still further into the future; but we must leave Ahab and his successors to a later chapter, and return to the beginning of Asa's long reign in Jerusalem.

Our Bible accounts give us plenty of figures for a time-line which would link the histories of the two kingdoms, though as the note at the end of this book indicates, they are less straightforward than they look. The time references in 2 Chronicles 15:19 – 16:1 pose one such problem. The 'thirty-sixth year' when Baasha fortified Ramah could not have been Year 36 of Asa's reign, as our present version says, for Baasha had died ten years before that. But it could have been Year 36 *since the kingdom was divided*; that would be Asa's Year 16, and its events would follow on seamlessly from those of his Year 15, as we shall see. If we take it that the original wording said something like that, everything else falls into place. What follows here is based on this assumption.

Asa's first ten years on the throne were a time of remarkable blessing. 'The land had rest. He had no war in those years, for the Lord gave him peace.' There was much building, much strengthening of defences. The nation's faith was revived, as the clutter of pagan religion was cleared away. Behind it all was Asa's determination that both he and his people should 'seek the Lord', looking constantly to Yahweh to follow his will and his way. After that wonderful decade – almost the days of Solomon come again – war clouds began to gather on the horizon, but a large, well-trained, well-equipped army was ready for whatever might come.

What did come in due course was another invasion from Egypt, where Shishak's successor Osorkon was now pharaoh. Commanded by his Sudanese general Zerah, an army twice the size of Asa's marched towards Judah's southern border. The hymn 'We rest on you, our Shield and our Defender' is based on Asa's confident prayer to Yahweh: 'We rest on you, and in your name we go'. They went, he and his forces, relying on the Lord, and came back victorious, laden with spoil. The prophet Azariah met them with a powerful message of encouragement. The religious revival was given a further boost, and Asa called a national assembly for the renewal of Judah's commitment to its God. It was his fifteenth year on the throne.

The news had spread like wildfire. 'Great numbers had deserted to him from Israel when they saw that the Lord his God was with him.' The substitute religion that Jeroboam had concocted for the northern tribes could not compete with this. For the first fifteen years of Asa's reign the two kingdoms had been ignoring each other, but Baasha could not allow such a haemorrhaging of Israel's population, and he moved to set up some sort of border control, in the vicinity of the town of Ramah, 'to prevent people leaving or entering Asa's domains'.

Then Asa did the strangest thing. Or perhaps it was not so strange. It is easy to slip from the heights to the depths. For years everything had gone right, now something was going wrong; and his reaction was either one of panic, or the automatic one of a scheming politician. (Even the saintly Asa could not trust his automatic responses always to be right ones.) He bribed Benhadad, king of Syria, to attack Baasha from the north, so as to create a diversion while the men of Judah dismantled the new fortifications along Israel's southern frontier and carted off the materials for their own defences.

Asa should of course have kept his nerve and trusted his God, as he had always done till then. Offering a bribe was wrong, funding it from the Temple treasury was sacrilegious, persuading Benhadad to break the treaty he had made with Baasha was disgraceful. Another prophet – his name was Hanani, perhaps the father of the prophet Jehu who brought an equally unwelcome word to Baasha – and another message from Yahweh to Asa, this time a rebuke and a punishment: for the next ten years, the rest of Baasha's reign, the pair of them would be involved in repeated border skirmishes. For the time being the days of peace were over.

Smarting from Hanani's harsh words, Asa reacted with anger, indeed cruelty, towards the prophet and his supporters. On a much later occasion, years afterwards and near the end of his life, his high standards would again slip and his faith would fail, when with his feet painfully diseased he looked for help only to his doctors and not to Yahweh. But from the way the Bible describes him and his times as a whole, that middle decade and those last two years of his reign were not characteristic. At heart, we are told, he was 'wholly true to the Lord all his days'. It is the first fifteen years, that is those that coincide with the first half of Baasha's reign, and then most of the last fifteen, while in Israel amid revolution and civil war and massacre five more northerners in turn claim the throne, – it is those years that show a king of Judah doing 'as David his father had done', and a kingdom blessed as Yahweh meant it to be.

IX

AS DIFFERENT AS CHALK AND CHEESE?

Although Asa did not always live up to his reputation as a king who ruled 'as David his father had done', and although his faith in Yahweh certainly faltered at the time of his last illness, he did look back to David's example as he planned the handover of power in Judah to his son Jehoshaphat. As we have seen, his famous ancestor – 'father' David was in our terms, of course, his great-great-grandfather – had set up a co-regency before he died, an overlap during which he and Solomon had ruled jointly. Asa, prompted perhaps by his failing health, decided in his last years to do likewise.

Jehoshaphat was by then in his thirties. His twenty-five-year reign – the co-regency was reckoned as the first three years of it – revealed him as one of the greatest of the Hebrew kings. Underlying all his achievements was the fact that the God of Israel was real to him, and figures repeatedly in his story. As he fortified strategic towns and built up a standing army, Yahweh was with him, Yahweh confirmed his rule, Yahweh directed his ways. Yahweh's law was the basis of his nationwide scheme of education,

Yahweh's name was held in awe by the nations around him; instead of picking fights with him they vied for his favours. He was rich, powerful, and much admired. His reign was in many ways not unlike Solomon's, though on a considerably smaller scale.

During the greater part of it, Judah's sister kingdom was ruled by a man who would be equally well remembered, but for all the opposite reasons: Ahab the son of Omri. The great difference had to do with the nation's religion. The northern crown had passed from one claimant to another, the seat of government had shifted from town to town, but one thing that had remained constant in Israel was that every king in turn stood by the religious policy of Jeroboam. Even the hapless Zimri, who had only seven days to do it in, could have been relied on to promise no changes in this respect, and perhaps even made some formal pledge to that effect.

Most of Omri's contemporaries saw his twelve years on the throne as a success story. But to the Bible writers it was the worst reign so far, and that of his son was going to be worse still. You can see why when you set 1 Kings 16:29-34, which introduces Ahab, alongside 2 Chronicles 17, which introduces Jehoshaphat; while the second passage is full of the name Yahweh, the first is full of the name Baal. It was bad enough for Jeroboam to have dreamt up a man-made religion and persuaded his people that this was the worship of Yahweh. Omri opened the door to an even greater evil. Alliances with the Phoenician seaport cities of Tyre and Sidon were high on his agenda, so it was no doubt he who proposed the marriage between Ahab and Jezebel, the daughter of the Sidonian king Ethbaal. She was a fervent devotee of Baal, the historic god of many of the Canaanite nations, and when Ahab came to the throne his wife brought her religion with her.

He was more than happy to go along with her ideas. He

decided that like that other hilltop city Jerusalem, with its temple of Yahweh, Israel's new capital Samaria should also have its temple, and Baal should be its god. Jezebel recruited and financed a horde of 'prophets' as propagandists for what began to look like the nation's official religion. Ahab shut his ears to the words of the true faith, and allowed her to set about a thorough purge of those who spoke up for it.

Baal was reckoned to be the giver of the rain that made the crops grow, the giver of fertility, in fact the giver of life. All he expected in return was the usual religious observances and donations, not tiresome things like justice and faithfulness and clean living. Indeed he positively encouraged self-indulgence: it was one of his main selling points. Yahweh, the true giver of life, was quite different – a God who loved his people, spoke with them, and expected high moral standards from them.

Israel's God was about to speak again. One of the wickedest of Israel's kings was brought face to face with one of the greatest of its prophets. Elijah simply appears, centre stage, with dramatic suddenness, and declares a word from Yahweh that neither Israel, nor Ahab, nor even Jezebel, will be able to shut their ears to. The word is *Drought*. As the seasons pass, further words from Yahweh will prove him to be all-powerful and Baal to be powerless. Having first decreed that rains shall fail and crops shall die, he then decrees that Elijah shall take refuge first in a remote corner of Ahab's kingdom and later in Jezebel's own homeland; that in each place the prophet shall be kept both alive and safely hidden; and that the drought shall end as and when Yahweh, not Baal, chooses. Yahweh, not Baal, is the God who gives – and takes – life.

All the words came true. Eventually, in a great meeting convened on Mount Carmel, overlooking the bay on which the modern city of Haifa stands, the whole company of Baal's prophets were challenged to get a public response from their god, and could not, while to the lone Elijah's simple prayer Yahweh returned a spectacular answer: not only his sacrificial bull, but even the altar on which it lay and the water with which both had been drenched, were vaporized by fire that fell from heaven. The assembly hailed Yahweh as the true God, the prophets of the false god were executed as the law of Moses demanded, and within the day, up from the western sea, the rains came.

What followed was a huge disappointment. Israel did not after all turn back to God; instead, Israel's queen laid plans to kill God's servant. Though the plans failed, Elijah came to see that his calling was not to lead the nation into spiritual renewal, but to be the spokesman for the faithful few within it, and the prophet of doom to their persecutors. Ahab and Jezebel meanwhile presided over a kingdom where injustice and oppression became increasingly the order of the day.

This is all a far cry from the picture we have of Judah through those same years. Jehoshaphat's name means 'Yahweh is Judge', and his people not only enjoyed prosperity and almost unbroken peace, but also benefited from his passionate concern for the rule of law, Yahweh's law, with courts set up and judges appointed in every town: justice for all. In this, in fact in almost everything, he and Ahab were as different as chalk and cheese.

So it is a shock to find the pair of them, on one memorable occasion, apparently the best of friends. It was all to do with the neighbouring kingdom of Aram, or Syria. Again unlike Jehoshaphat, Ahab often had to send his troops into action. While in earlier times Israelite kings, and the judges before them, were repeatedly harassed by their Philistine neighbours to the south west, for Ahab trouble generally came from the Arameans on his north-eastern frontier. Very recently, however, he and Benhadad, their king, had agreed a truce, in the face of a common threat. The ancient kingdom of Assyria (in today's Iraq) had revived after long obscurity, and its armies had twice driven westwards as far as the Mediterranean coast. A third invasion was met by the united forces of a dozen western nations, and held to a draw at Qarqar on the River Orontes in Syria.

The year was 853, and though he did not know it Ahab had little time to live. He was to be given one last chance to mend his ways. In a matter of months the allies felt secure enough to start squabbling among themselves again. Another battle was about to be joined, much nearer home, between Ahab and Benhadad. Ahab was eager to recapture the Israelite town of Ramoth Gilead, some way east of the Jordan and on an important trade route, which had been for too long in the hands of the Arameans. He had begun to get the upper hand in earlier clashes with Benhadad, but to be sure of winning this one he put out feelers for a possible ally, and invited Jehoshaphat to Samaria for a state visit.

Times had changed. Hostilities between the two Hebrew kingdoms were a thing of the past. It now suited both parties, for different reasons, to stress what they had in common instead of the questions of religion that divided them. Amid pomp and ceremony and lavish entertainment Ahab broached the subject of a joint campaign. Jehoshaphat, no doubt hoping that he might somehow be an influence for good, agreed to it heartily. Were they not all Israelites? Though of course, he went on, for God's people to embark on such a venture they ought to have it confirmed by one of God's prophets.

Samaria was able to produce not one, but four hundred and one, all of whom said what each king wanted to hear: Ahab, that the campaign should go ahead; Jehoshaphat, that this was Yahweh saying so. The four-hundred-and-first prophet, however, the only true man of God among them, added that if they did go Ahab would not come back.

Five times already during his reign the patient God of Israel had spoken directly to Ahab, and this would be his last chance to repent and obey. But stubborn to the end, he went ahead with his cherished scheme. In the battle he tried to outwit destiny by disguising himself as a common soldier, but a stray Syrian arrow struck him through a crack in his armour, and by sundown he had bled to death.

Jehoshaphat narrowly escaped a similar fate. Were he and Ahab really as different as chalk and cheese? He too should not have gone to Ramoth Gilead. He too had his cherished ideas, and on three separate occasions he made a fool of himself by pressing on with a harebrained scheme of which Yahweh disapproved. The unity of Israel was a great ideal, but it could never consist of some sort of contrived union between the House of David and whichever dynasty happened to be ruling the renegade north. Jehoshaphat seems to have thought it could. First he had made a marriage alliance with the House of Omri, between his son Jehoram and Ahab's daughter Athaliah, which had the direst long-term results. Then there was this military alliance with Ahab, which nearly cost him his life; and after that he would make a commercial alliance with Ahab's son Ahaziah, joining him to build an ocean-going fleet at the Red Sea port of Ezion Geber. Yahweh, as patient with him as he had been with Ahab, duly wrecked the ships, in the hope that the dear man might at last learn his lesson.

For he *was* dear to his God. That was the basic difference between the two kings. It was not unlike the difference between Saul and David. Ahab had the occasional fit of remorse, but was at heart a self-willed rebel against God. Jehoshaphat had the occasional foolish lapse, but was at heart a man who wanted to know and follow the ways of Yahweh.

Two events late in his reign, both military actions

against the kingdom of Moab, leave us with this picture of him. Ahab's successor Ahaziah had already been succeeded by Jehoram, and the prophet Elijah by his protégé Elisha; both of these will come to the fore in our next chapter. Moab, which had been subject to Israel, made a bid for independence, Jehoram asked Judah's help in crushing the revolt, and Jehoshaphat gave it (again!). When the coalition faced seeming defeat, a miracle-working word from Elisha turned the tables. But the Moabites were not crushed. They returned, this time to take revenge on Judah. This second campaign threatened total disaster, until Jehoshaphat led all his people first 'to seek the Lord' – 'we do not know what to do, but our eyes are on you,' they cried – and then to march out to face the enemy, only to find that Moab and its allies had turned on one another in a fury of destruction, and there was no one left to fight. It was a famous victory for a man and a nation that knew and trusted the God of Israel.

X

THE LEGACY OF AHAB

Jehoshaphat died in 848, at the age of sixty. We have to backtrack five years or so to see what had happened after Ahab was killed at Ramoth Gilead. He left a complicated legacy of trouble not only for Israel but also for Judah, and indeed for us who try to get clear in our minds the events and people of those middle years of the ninth century.

The most obvious complication has to do with names. Was not Jehoram Jehoshaphat's son, and crown prince of Judah? How come, then, that he seems to be the king – the king of *Israel* – who later invites Jehoshaphat to join his campaign against the Moabites?

Well, there were two of him. Even more confusing, the next two kings in the south were called Jehoram and Ahaziah, while the next two in the north were Ahaziah and Jehoram. It is almost as though that odd couple, the 'chalk and cheese' contemporaries with whom our last chapter was concerned, were godfathers to each other's children, bandying compliments at the font. Both names include the name of Israel's God; in English Bibles, the 'jeh-' of one and the '-iah' of the other represent the Yahweh in whom Jehoshaphat did believe, and in whom Ahab would say he believed when it suited him to do so.

It was about the time of Ahab's death that in the south Jehoram of Judah was made co-regent with his father, repeating the pattern of the previous generation, when for a short time Asa and Jehoshaphat had together ruled Judah twenty years earlier. This prince was, as we know, married to Ahab's daughter, so it was his brother-in-law, her brother Ahaziah, who in 853 succeeded to the throne of the northern kingdom.

The late king of Israel would have been proud of his son and heir. Ahaziah turned out to be not only as deaf to the inconvenient words of Yahweh, and as drawn to the much more comfortable religion of Baal, as Ahab had been, but also equally good at twisting the gullible Jehoshaphat round his little finger – witness the proposed joint trading venture at Ezion Geber. Fortunately his reign was going to be a good deal shorter than he or anyone else expected.

Elijah, the chief, if not the only, public spokesman for the old faith of Israel, the mouthpiece for Yahweh's messages, was still around. Kings might come and go, but as a later prophet would say, 'the word of our God will stand for ever'. He confronted Ahaziah as he had first confronted Ahab, appearing as if from nowhere with a doom-laden prediction. The king had fallen from a palace balcony, and being seriously injured wanted to know if God would heal him. For him, 'God' meant neither of the Yahwehs, whether the newer one in Bethel or the original one in Jerusalem, nor even the Baal in Samaria, but the Baal who was worshipped miles away in the Philistine city of Ekron, and perhaps was thought to specialize in healings. Towards Ekron therefore the royal messengers set out, returning much too soon, greatly embarrassed, on the orders of someone even more authoritative than

Ahaziah, with the message that the king would not recover. Who would be so daring? 'A wild hairy man,' they said. Elijah! This was not to be borne. A posse of fifty men was dispatched to capture him. By some trickery, it seemed, 'fire from heaven' destroyed them, and the next company that went out too. (Who sent the 'fire from heaven' on Mount Carmel, Ahaziah?) Finally Elijah marched into Samaria, very obviously uncaptured and with the third fifty trooping behind him sheepish but alive, to repeat Yahweh's message of doom. Ahab had been given many chances to repent; this was Ahaziah's only one. He was a lost cause from the start. 'He died according to the word of the Lord', in only his second year on the throne, and was succeeded by his brother Jehoram.

So now in the south Jehoram of Judah rules alongside his father for the closing years of Jehoshaphat's reign, while Jehoram of Israel has become king in the north. And about this time Elisha takes over Elijah's role as the great prophet of God's people. The older man is removed from the scene by Yahweh, and passes his mantle, literally, to the younger, whose path will cross that of the new king, as Elijah's crossed Ahab's, on three or four significant occasions.

For Elisha to be seen from then on wearing the cloak Elijah had left behind would have been a sign that he was taking forward the same work. He too spoke out for Yahweh without fear or favour. He too made Yahweh's presence felt through the things he did. But his career was in some ways bigger than Elijah's. He travelled more widely, met more people, both high and low, dealt out more blessings and more punishments, became known as a miracle-worker; far from disappearing into the desert for long periods, he openly moved around the country as his great predecessor Samuel had done, and even had a home in Samaria City. Centuries afterwards, a man named John would emerge from desert places, reminding people of Elijah by his wild looks and fierce preaching. Did it perhaps occur to some in Israel in those later times that John's cousin Jesus followed him with a career not unlike that of Elisha?

The Bible account may not be telling the Elisha stories in the order they happened, but it does give us a good impression of the many ups and downs of the twelve-year reign of Jehoram of Israel. This tallied almost exactly with that of his brother-in-law and namesake, Jehoram of Judah, first co-regent and then sole king in Jerusalem. The latter Jehoram, Jehoshaphat's son, must have been a great disappointment to his father, for 'he walked in the way of the kings of Israel' and 'did what was evil in the sight of the Lord.' But it was Jehoshaphat's own fault, for arranging the marriage between his son and Ahab's daughter. That was how the legacy of Ahab's wickedness spread across the border from Israel to Judah. The two Jehorams were birds of a feather.

In fact Jehoshaphat would have been not just disappointed, but horrified beyond words, if he had known the kind of king his son was going to be. Jehoram of Judah added to the wickedness of his northern in-laws a bloodthirsty policy that looked back to the days of their predecessors Baasha and Zimri: he made sure of his throne by murdering all his six brothers. They were soon avenged. To Philistine and Arabian invaders he lost much of his property, his wives, and (appropriately) all his sons. All, that is, except the youngest. Yahweh would make sure that the House of David continued, even though this traitor to its traditions would be justly punished; just as the House of Omri was doomed, even if the last of its kings sometimes showed a grudging admiration for Elisha. Also, in due course, Jehoram of Judah lost both his health and the respect of his people. He died of a gruesome disease of the bowels, and they gave him a very cut-price funeral. No one was sorry to see him go.

During the reigns of the two Jehorams, through much of the 840s, it was as well that Israel was on good terms with its southern neighbour, because things were very different along its northern frontier. We know how the grand alliance that briefly united Israel and Syria, together with several other western states, for the battle of Qarqar, quickly fell apart, and how hostilities between the two nations soon began again. We know too how Israel's attempt then to recapture the town of Ramoth Gilead failed. The army of Benhadad, the Syrian king, would have been commanded by his famous general Naaman; and the Bible says matter-of-factly that just as it was Yahweh who enticed Ahab to his death there, so it was Yahweh, not the Syrian god Rimmon, who gave Naaman the victory. The God of Israel was no mere one-nation deity, but the only God in all the earth, as Naaman himself was one day going to describe him.

A few years later, on into the reign of Jehoram of Israel, when Elisha had become a familiar and respected figure in and around Samaria, the 'war' had come to mean no more than the occasional border raid. In the course of one such raid an Israelite girl was captured, and back in Syria became Naaman's wife's maid. When the great general contracted an incurable skin complaint, the youngster could not help saying something to her mistress about Elisha's reputation. By that time there was an uneasy truce, and Naaman was able to visit the prophet in Samaria, and to experience a remarkable cure.

Then there was a time when relations between Samaria and Damascus cooled yet again, and Syrian forces began to make inroads into Israelite territory, only to find their plans discovered and made known to Jehoram by Elisha. The Israelite king, very appreciative of this help, was less pleased when another Syrian invasion got as far as besieging Samaria, so effectively as to cause serious famine in the city. But there too Yahweh was in control, and the siege was lifted suddenly and miraculously when Elisha said it would be. Jehoram really had no excuse for his unbelief.

Elisha had two more tasks before this last king of the House of Omri was removed. It was 843, and had they known it both Jehorams had only two years to live, when Yahweh sent his prophet off to Damascus. Whatever the political situation, Elisha personally was as respected in Syria as he was in Israel, and the Syrian king Benhadad, who was sick, was as eager to consult this servant of Israel's God as Ahaziah of Israel had been to consult a Philistine Baal ten years before. An ironic cross-over! Benhadad sent Hazael, one of his staff, laden with gifts, to ask the question Ahaziah had asked: would he get better?

Elisha recognized the messenger's name. Hazael? Next king of Syria, next scourge of my faithless people Israel, Yahweh had once said to Elijah. Now it fell to Elisha to tell Hazael so. Benhadad's illness did not trouble him long. The following day Hazael smothered the sick man with a wet cloth, took the kingdom, and started up the war machine once more.

Yet again Ramoth Gilead was the bone of contention, and again Israel and Judah went out as allies against the Syrians. A new king had come to the throne in the southern kingdom. This was the other Ahaziah, the only surviving son of Jehoram of Judah, who had just died his unpleasant death, and the nephew of Jehoram of Israel. Apparently Ahaziah had not taken part in the fighting against Hazael, and he came to visit his uncle Jehoram, who had, and had been wounded in it. These two met in the palace at Jezreel, where Ahab's widow Jezebel was still living. Whatever important matters of state they may have been discussing, their talks would turn out to be a waste of breath. Ahab's family had sown the wind, and was about to reap the whirlwind. More of the evils of his legacy were to be worked out, through two other people in two other places:

Athaliah, the queen mother of Judah, down in Jerusalem, and across in Ramoth Gilead a high-ranking officer in the army of Israel named Jehu. One task remained of those Elijah had handed down to his successor.

XI

A BLOOD-BATH

Elijah to be replaced by Elisha, Benhadad by Hazael, Jehoram by Jehu. That is Yahweh's scenario. The story he writes is not only that of his servants the prophets, but also that of the rulers of the nations, those who don't worship him as well as those who do. He is the 'disposer supreme and judge of the earth'.

The first replacement has already happened, and Elisha has been to Damascus and set up the second one. There remains the third matter, the succession in Israel, where the last king of the House of Omri, Jehoram, is about to be removed. This will not, even now, be the end of Ahab's legacy, for his daughter married the other Jehoram and has six more years in which to lord it over Judah, where the House of David is supposed to be ruling. But in the northern kingdom a bloody revolution is about to be unleashed. Elisha has deputed a student from the prophets' Training College to find Jehu, one of the Israelite commanders defending Ramoth Gilead (currently in their hands) against the Syrians, and to anoint him as the new king of Israel.

Because of the events that were to follow, we need to remember what this anointing was. Oil poured on the head by a prophet of the Lord was the ceremony by which Saul and David and Solomon had been marked out as Yahweh's chosen kings. The Bible notes no such anointing of any foreigner except Hazael, or of any northerner except Jehu. Yahweh had chosen these men to be the means by which he would punish the House of Omri, and Ahab's family in particular.

The Israelite army's high command was gathered probably in a courtyard of the citadel in Ramoth Gilead when Elisha's messenger arrived. Though Jehu and his colleagues may not have known who he was, they did know what he was. There was something recognizable about a prophet; from his look and his manner, you might call him (as they did) a 'mad fellow'. But you would be foolish to ignore what he said.

In this case what he had to say was a personal message for Jehu, who excused himself from the meeting and took the visitor indoors. Within minutes the young man re-emerged, his mission accomplished, and ran off as fast as his legs would carry him. He had good reason to believe that he had dropped a lighted match into a powder keg. As soon as Jehu also came out, his fellow-officers clamoured to know what had happened. He must have wondered how much he should tell them. They could see the oil on his head, they would take a prophet's word seriously, they felt no great loyalty to Jehoram. So: 'Yahweh has anointed me king over Israel,' he said.

That was enough. Down went their cloaks for a royal carpet on the courtyard steps, the trumpets blew, and the shout was raised: 'Jehu is king!'

The prophet had in fact said rather more than this. He had spelt out the purpose of the anointing, which was that through Jehu the House of Ahab and its destructive policies should themselves be destroyed. The new king was quite ruthless enough for the task. And there was something else about him. How might he prevent Jehoram's being warned of what was afoot, and given the chance to escape? By getting to Jezreel himself before anyone else could. As well as ruthlessness, he had a famously furious turn of speed as a charioteer.

At Jezreel, as we know, he would find not only Ahab's son but also his grandson Ahaziah, king of Judah, and his widow Jezebel. The watchman on the town walls spied the company of chariots and horsemen approaching fast: 'It must be General Jehu, he's driving like a madman.' (It was the word the officers had used to describe the prophet. The coming together of these two 'mad' characters certainly was proving explosive.) The two kings, uncle and nephew, assumed that there was important news from Ramoth Gilead – they were right, though it was not the kind of news they were expecting – and they set out to meet him.

The two parties were within earshot of each other when Jehoram realized, from the shouted response to his shouted question, that Jehu was coming not as his servant but as his executioner. They were also within bowshot, and Jehoram had only the time to pull his horses round in a tight U-turn and call a warning to Ahaziah before Jehu's arrow struck him between the shoulders and killed him instantly. A second arrow hit Ahaziah as he also turned to flee, though he was only wounded; his soldiers got him as far as Megiddo, but there he too died.

The queen mother was next. Jehu entered Jezreel without opposition. Jezebel looked out of an upper window in the palace, and divined at once what was happening. She was able to tell Jehu in a few well-chosen words what she thought of him, before some of the palace staff, hastily changing sides as the situation obviously demanded, threw her down to her death.

Jehu's breakneck drive had got him to Jezreel quicker than any rumour could have travelled. Now, however, with two kings and a queen dead, he was happy for rumour to take over, and spread the news of the coup for him. So by the time official letters signed 'Jehu' arrived in Samaria, the leading citizens of the capital were already terrified of the name, and only too eager to fall in with the new king's orders: the elimination of every person connected with Ahab who might possibly dispute Jehu's claim to the throne. When eventually he came himself, he would amend that to 'every connection of Ahab's, period,' and even more heads would roll.

He did not hesitate to add to his death-list a large group of members of Judah's royal family. On his way to Samaria he had met this party, which was travelling to Jezreel to visit its relatives in the north and had not yet learned about recent events. 'Take them alive,' commanded Jehu, and his soldiers, understanding him perfectly, 'took them alive – and slaughtered them.' The killings were turning into a massacre. But Jehu was still not finished. The biggest blood-bath of all was yet to come.

Whether or not they believed God to be behind this revolution, most people were taking for granted that it was a matter of politics, not religion. Jehu was very willing that they should continue to think so for the time being. He knew differently, of course. He knew through the prophets that he had been chosen to rid Israel not only of Ahab's family but also of the Baal-religion it had introduced with such enthusiasm. His publicity, however, said just the opposite. There would be a national celebration in honour of Baal, all Baal's priests and prophets and every true worshipper would be there, those who clung obstinately to the faith of Yahweh would not be welcome. The day came, the great temple in Samaria was crammed with people, the new king presided and the sacrificial animals were slaughtered. Then he left, and the real object of the exercise became clear as his soldiers moved in and the human slaughter began. When not a man remained alive, the building too was destroyed, and 'thus Jehu stamped out the worship of Baal in Israel.'

Something similar, though on a much smaller scale, happened about the same time in Judah. It stemmed from the ill-advised alliance between the two kingdoms by which Ahab's daughter had married Jehoshaphat's son. We remember that when Jehoshaphat died all his sons had perished too, all except this one, Jehoram of Judah, who had himself ordered the massacre of his brothers so as to secure his own position. Then – it was poetic justice – all his sons were killed also, by Philistine invaders, though again with one exception. That was the Ahaziah of Judah who in due course succeeded to the throne on Jehoram's death, and who now, very soon afterwards, had been killed by Jehu. His mother Athaliah, Ahab's daughter, was still very much alive; and when the news of his murder reached Jerusalem she acted at once. Yet again, for the third time in three generations, a king's sons were to die. For what she set out to do was not to make sure that the eldest of Ahaziah's boys took his place as king, nor to proclaim herself regent alongside the young man, nor even to vow vengeance on Jehu, but instead to embark on a killing spree of her own, disposing now of all her grandsons in order to take the crown herself; as we shall see in our next chapter. The plan was horrifying and quite inexcusable, to say nothing of its threat to the promise Yahweh had made to David that the line of his descendants would never be destroyed.

Even so, there had been far more bloodshed in Israel than in Judah, and it may seem to us not only paradoxical, but also very strange, that while the comparatively few killings in the south were the work of people who cared nothing for Yahweh, Jehu's many killings were done in Yahweh's name. Was the God of Israel really sponsoring mass murder?

If we could ask Yahweh's prophets for an explanation in modern terms, they might well say that the House of Ahab, with all the evils for which it was responsible, was like a cancer destroying the nation; whereas Jehu was like a surgeon destroying the cancer, and having to deal also with the secondary growths that had spread throughout the body of Israel.

Athaliah, secure on the throne in Jerusalem (or so she thought), was beyond even Jehu's reach. But time would tell.

That year, 840, had been an eventful one. It saw the end of the longest-running dynasty so far in the northern kingdom, that of Omri and Ahab and two of Ahab's sons, and what looked like the end of the whole Davidic line of kings in the south. It saw the rooting out of a false religion, and a great deal of bloodshed.

Things were not what they seemed in Judah, as we shall discover in our next chapter. But in Israel Jehu's revolution had two far-reaching effects, one positive and one negative. Because he had abolished Baal worship so thoroughly, Yahweh promised him a dynasty that would last even longer than Omri's, covering five generations, five reigns, and ninety years. In contrast, he never lifted a finger to deal with the travesty of Yahweh worship that had tainted the northern kingdom since the days of Jeroboam. Because of that, he was promised ongoing trouble throughout his 28-year reign from the ever-increasing power of Hazael, whose Aramean forces occupied great swathes of Israelite territory to the north and east. Ironically, one of Jehu's first losses would have been Ramoth Gilead, the town where he had been proclaimed king.

What are we to make of him? Not a nice man, we may think, though a very efficient one. Certainly he did have not much in the way of spiritual perception. If he presumed that obeying Yahweh in one matter left him free to disobey in another, he was sadly mistaken.

XII

YOUNG KING, OLD PROPHET

'The kings of the earth set themselves against the Lord and against his Anointed One: "Let us break their bonds," they say, "and throw off their fetters."' Ever since it was first written, perhaps in the early days of the Israelite monarchy, the poem we know as Psalm 2 has been a reminder of two great facts about Israel's God, Yahweh, the 'invisible king' of our first chapter. One is that governments, and powerful people generally, tend to have ideas of their own, and to refuse to be bound by what Yahweh says. The other fact is that over against them he has appointed a deputy of his choosing, a viceroy, whose reign has already begun, though they seldom recognize it. And the psalm states almost in so many words that Yahweh is going to have the last laugh.

Athaliah, 'that wicked woman' as the Bible calls her, was one of these rebellious rulers. With Ahab as her father and Jezebel as her mother (or stepmother), she had been brought up to believe in Baal, and when she moved south to marry Jehoram of Judah she brought Baal worship with her. She set up some kind of Baal-temple in Jerusalem, and helped herself to the treasures of the temple of Yahweh to furnish it. She for one was not going to be in bondage to this Israelite God.

When her husband died and their son Ahaziah succeeded to the throne, she became queen mother. In the monarchies of that time and place this was a position of considerable power, and she made the most of it. But then a still grander possibility opened up before her. For the position of the other kind of ruler, the anointed king in Jerusalem spoken of by Psalm 2, seemed to become more and more uncertain. The anointing was for none but a prince of the House of David, and Athaliah had twice seen a king of Judah die leaving only one possible successor. Now that her son also had died, one of the first victims of Jehu's coup, she could make sure that this time there would be no successors at all, and take the throne for herself, if she were sufficiently callous and resolute.

She was. Orders went out for the murder of all her grandsons. The promise of Yahweh would fail, the line of David would end. Though Jehu had wiped out the House of Ahab in the north, it would be reborn in the south as the House of Athaliah. The beast with the mortal wound (as the final book of the Bible would put it long afterwards) would live again.

Yahweh's plans, however, were not so easily thwarted. Providence both general and particular saw to that. After so many good years under the God-fearing kings Asa and Jehoshaphat, there had been general disgust in the southern kingdom at the doings of Jehoram, and its people had rallied round the spiritual leadership of their high priest Jehoiada. And the particular twist in the tale was that the high priest had actually married a sister of the murdered king Ahaziah. This woman, Jehosheba, deplored her parents' wickedness. Having a foot in both camps, she got wind of the queen's plan to destroy every claimant to the throne, and was able to spirit away the youngest of her brother's children, a baby not twelve months old. When the royal death-squad came round to slaughter these innocents (this too was a preview of something that would figure in the New Testament, centuries later), little Joash was safely hidden in one of the temple store-rooms. In fact in the temple he remained for the next six years, cared for by some loyal family among the resident staff, perhaps that of the high priest himself. The few who knew were sworn to secrecy.

So too was a far larger number, when in the child's seventh year Jehoiada judged the time was right for a showdown. He was a remarkable man. No other priest of Israel could have done what he did – not Zadok or Abiathar, certainly not Eli – and he did it so quietly and quickly that Athaliah knew nothing of it till she heard the cheering of the armed throng that filled the temple courts. When she came storming in from the palace, she realized that she was the victim of some sort of coup, as her brother in the north had been, and guessed at once who the small boy with a crown on his head, up there by the pillar, must be. In her fury, it did not occur to her how pointless, and how ironic, was her cry of 'Treason!' It was she, not Jehoiada, who was guilty of treason, 'against the Lord and against his Anointed One', and as a murderous traitor they executed her. With her death the House of Ahab finally perished.

There were no such upheavals in Samaria, where the House of Jehu was by now firmly in control. In the bloodthirsty coup of 840 its first king had made short work of all possible rivals, and set up a dynasty that would last for nearly a hundred years, through the rest of the ninth century and halfway into the eighth.

But Jehu was much less successful in coping with threats from outside Israel. Scarcely had he come to the throne when Assyria began to flex its muscles again, and

Shalmaneser III once more marched westwards to terrorize the smaller kingdoms along the Mediterranean coast. This time they made no attempt at a united front to oppose the invader, and Jehu along with the rest grovelled before him – carvings on the 'Black Obelisk' in the British Museum show our hero doing literally that – and paid him handsomely to go away.

Less frightening but more damaging were the unfriendly schemes of Hazael of Damascus. It was another irony that he and Jehu, each made king by an unlikely anointing from Yahweh, should find themselves so often at loggerheads. The northern kingdom's borderlands were repeatedly harassed, some indeed overrun and occupied, by Hazael's troops. For most of the forty-odd years in which first Jehu and then his son Jehoahaz ruled, Aram grew ever more aggressive and Israel ever feebler, till in contrast to the two thousand chariots that Ahab had been able to send against the Assyrians at Qarqar in 853, Jehoahaz could mobilize no more than ten; the record tells us that 'the king of Aram had destroyed the rest.'

Jehu, when he learned at the beginning of his reign of the approach of Shalmaneser's armies, must have reacted with dismay; but to Jehoahaz, at the end of his, the news of yet another Assyrian invasion came as a positive relief. 'Yahweh provided a deliverer for Israel', says the Bible, and his name was Adad-nirari III – one more godless 'strong man' made to serve the purposes of the true God, for he targeted Aram and its capital Damascus, and broke the power of the Aramean kings. That however still lay in the future, in the last decade of the century.

Looked at from Yahweh's point of view, the Hebrew kingdoms presented during those years a kind of mirror image of each other. In Israel, the man-made religion invented by Jeroboam still held sway, but at any rate two good things happened: first the dreadful Baal worship that Jezebel had introduced was rooted out, and then the misery caused by Aram's repeated attacks made people turn back to Yahweh for help. By contrast, in Judah it was the true faith that still held sway, but in spite of this two bad things happened; and for both, sad to say, King Joash was responsible.

He had been greatly blessed, having been saved from death as a baby by the godly Jehosheba and brought up by her husband the high priest, who for the rest of his long life was the young king's guide and mentor. Joash was given the opportunity to carry out a thorough restoration of the Jerusalem temple after the damage Athaliah had done, and he took it wholeheartedly. But in the latter part of his reign, after Jehoiada had died, things went wrong. The first blot on his character is recorded in 2 Kings 12, the second in 2 Chronicles 24. One was foolish, the other was wicked.

If ever Judah had assumed it was safe from attack by Aram because Israel lay between them as a buffer, the idea evaporated some time in the early 800s. Hazael's armies had long since annexed Israelite lands all down the east side of the Jordan, and now set out from their Syrian home base to rampage down the coast to the west of the two little kingdoms. They captured the ancient Philistine city of Gath, then turned inland and marched on Jerusalem. Joash in a panic forgot all he had learned about the power of Yahweh to protect his own, and ransacked the treasures of the recently-restored temple to buy off the invaders.

Later came something worse – a wicked sin that led to a wicked crime. The old pagan religion was allowed to creep back in, and a prophet brave enough to speak out against this was murdered. And each deed in turn was sponsored, believe it or not, by the king himself. Retribution was swift, again at the hands of the Arameans. It was a relatively small number of enemy troops that came this time, says the Chronicler; Hazael had died, the latest Assyrian invasion had humbled his successor Ben-hadad, and the power of Aram was a shadow of its former self; but even so, outside the gates of Jerusalem 'Yahweh delivered into their hands a much larger army.' Defeated and badly hurt, Joash took to his bed, and there he died – not of his wounds, but assassinated by two traitors among his own staff.

The year was 796. Joash's northern contemporary Jehoahaz had died a couple of years earlier, and been succeeded by his son, another Joash (this time we shall avoid confusion by spelling the northerner's name Jehoash). The kingdom of Aram had been pronounced dead, but was not yet willing to lie down, as we know from the account of its attacks on Jerusalem. One person who was certainly not dead, though we have not heard of him for some time, was the prophet Elisha. Jehoash, like many others before him, high and low, revered this great man, now stricken by his last illness. Did the new king have a superstitious hope that his faithless nation might yet be defended by the mere presence of this servant of Yahweh, formidable even in his old age? Was Elisha, like his predecessor Elijah, 'the chariots and horsemen of Israel'? But if so, what would happen when he died? Jehoash went to consult him.

'Shoot an arrow from the window,' commanded the old man. The king did as he was told, aiming eastwards towards enemy-occupied Transjordan; and that, said the prophet, signified victory over Aram. As for the remaining arrows, he continued, the ground is the place for them; probably meaning not that Jehoash should strike them against the floor, but that he should shoot them out of the window into the ground: that is where your enemies will end up.

Again Jehoash did as he was told; but three times only, and Elisha was vexed. Only the confidence to expect three victories, when the Aramean threat might have been removed completely! Would he ever find real enthusiasm for the cause of Yahweh among these northern tribes?

Still, at least the king had come to the right person for help. Yahweh's ancient promises to Abraham and his descendants held good even now, and, as in the days of Elijah, there was still a remnant, even here, who believed that.

XIII

THE THISTLE AND THE CEDAR

A review and a recap are going to be helpful at this point as we follow the story of the Old Testament kings.

After Rehoboam's kingdom had broken in two, back in the tenth century, the most significant thing that distinguished the half that he kept from the half that fell to Jeroboam was the religious difference between them.

In those days, as we know, religion was central to the life of every nation. Everyone believed in some sort of god. For both the Hebrew kingdoms, 'God' meant Yahweh, the One who had made them his own people when his servant Moses rescued them from Egypt. King David had planned a temple for this God in Jerusalem, and King Solomon had built it, and that was the spiritual centre of Israel, which posed a problem for Jeroboam. How could his subjects be politically loyal to his government in the north while their religious loyalty was still to Rehoboam's temple in the south?

His solution was to create a sort of northern clone of that southern sanctuary and the religion that went with it. All the trappings of the worship of Yahweh down there had their equivalents up here. So the two systems looked alike. That was the object of the exercise. The difference was that Judah's religion had come from Yahweh himself, while its rival was a man-made imitation, invented by Jeroboam.

Jehoshaphat, who inherited the throne of Judah sixty years later, was a big-hearted man, willing to think the best of everybody. He regretted the fact that Israel was divided. He could not imagine how it might be reunited, but he hoped at any rate to foster good relations between the sister kingdoms, even when his contemporary Ahab was diluting his people's faith still further by letting his wife Jezebel bring in a Canaanite religion several degrees worse than Jeroboam's.

Jehoshaphat was trying to repair the damage done by his great-grandfather Rehoboam. His six-times-great-grandmother, Ruth the Moabitess, had thrown in her lot with her Israelite in-laws with the memorable words, 'Wherever you go, I will go; your people shall be my people, and your God my God.' He responded with similar words to an invitation from Ahab, though he could not quite bring himself to echo Ruth's 'Your God my God'. (Was Ahab's God *really* Yahweh?)

The curious thing was that this alliance between Judah and Israel, which fudged their differences over who God was, and so was based on very shaky foundations, seemed on the whole, and at first, to work pretty well. It led to co-operation against common enemies around their borders, and to the complicated game of inter-marrying and name-swapping that was such a feature of the two royal houses in the mid-ninth century.

Now, however, as the eighth century dawned, this cosy relationship seemed less important. There was much less of the pressure from outside which had brought the kingdoms together. The Aramean kings in Damascus had been brought low by Assyria, and then the Assyrian king himself had disappeared from the scene, drawn away by problems back in his home country. We have already noticed how one more pair of namesakes overlapped briefly; the reign of Jehoash of Israel began in 797, a year or two before the reign of Joash of Judah came to an end (the names are the same, and can be spelt either way). But Jehoash and Amaziah, the new king in Jerusalem, had no plans for a partnership like that between Ahab and Jehoshaphat.

Jehoash was not the sort of person who would look to Yahweh's prophets for day-to-day guidance. But he had been glad enough to have Elisha, one of the greatest of them, living in his kingdom, if only as a talisman or insurance policy, and had been dismayed to hear that the great man was on his deathbed. He remembered the arrows he had been told to shoot from Elisha's window when he had gone to visit him, and the victories that they had signified did happen. Three times he led his armies out against the weakened power of Aram, and recaptured the towns that the Arameans had taken from Israel when Hazael was their king.

Amaziah too was keen to win back territories on the east side of the Jordan that had formerly been ruled by his predecessors. Far to the south of the area where Jehoash had been campaigning lay the mountainous country of Edom, once part of David's empire. It was on this land that Amaziah had set his sights. But he knew the project would be no walk-over. The Edomites, having long since regained their independence, intended to keep it. The modern tourist trail to Petra, the 'rose-red city half as old as time', gives a good idea of Edom's difficult terrain, rugged and easily defended. Accordingly, Amaziah decided that he would have to increase the size of his army.

Jehoash must have won his battles against Aram by this time, since a considerable number of his troops were free to hire themselves out as mercenaries when they heard of Amaziah's recruitment drive. The scheme did not work as planned. A 'man of God', a prophet, warned the king not to use these extra troops, coming as they did from the godless north. Under Yahweh's banner his own small army would be quite capable of defeating Edom – and, incidentally, the expense he had been put to in hiring the mercenaries would be more than repaid. So it turned out: both in the valley south of the Dead Sea, and in the rocky heights above it, the Edomite forces were destroyed, and Amaziah came home with a great deal of plunder.

But the seeds of his own destruction were being sown. Among the spoils of war he had brought back to Jerusalem were images of the pagan gods worshipped in Edom, and for some reason best known to himself he too bowed down and burned incense before them. A second prophet came to remonstrate with him, and was rudely rebuffed. Like Saul long before, he had disregarded the word of Yahweh, and his fate was sealed.

Disappointed of its share of the booty, the contingent from Israel that Amaziah had dismissed had taken out its frustration on the towns of Judah by looting those that it passed on its way home. Amaziah, seeking reparation for this outrage, demanded a face-to-face meeting with Jehoash. The latter saw himself as very much the better man. He reckoned that Amaziah's victory over Edom had gone to his head, and told him so by sending a message that consisted of a little story. We might picture it as a strip cartoon: Frame 1 – a very grand cedar of Lebanon is looking down on a diminutive, but prickly, thistle; Frame 2 – the thistle proposes a marriage alliance between their two great families (!); Frame 3 – some passing forest creature treads on the thistle. Enough said?

Amaziah was offended, and declared war. He got his
face-to-face meeting, but it was not the kind he intended.
Jehoash invaded, and captured him on his own territory.
He was first taken back to Jerusalem, where he had the
mortification of seeing part of the city's walls demolished
before his eyes, and both palace and temple ransacked,
and then (it seems, though the details are not clear) was
carried off with other hostages to Samaria.

This left Judah with a problem. It was a monarchy
whose monarch was for the foreseeable future detained
elsewhere. Its leading citizens decided, and everyone else
agreed, that something like the principle of co-regency
was called for. A few years before he died Asa had made
his son Jehoshaphat his co-regent, and Jehoshaphat had
done the same with his son Jehoram. In this case Amaziah
had no say in the matter, but the nation decided to bring
forward a version of this regency arrangement and make
his son Uzziah 'king' in his place, at any rate for the time
being.

Uzziah (in 2 Kings his name is spelt Azariah) was
sixteen years old. In Samaria, Jehoash had himself already
made his own son Jeroboam his co-regent – it was the
first and only time such a thing would happen in the
north – and between them these two northern kings were
going to make the first half of the eighth century the most
prosperous period in their kingdom's history. No doubt
Jehoash, holding Amaziah as a hostage, saw the untried
prince who had been unexpectedly voted on to the throne
in Jerusalem as little more than another thistle, likely to
be as easily trodden down as his father had been.

In this Jehoash was to be proved very wrong. But so far
as Amaziah was concerned, the rest of his life was a sorry
tale. During his first five years on the throne of Judah, he
had thought he could pick and choose which messages
from Yahweh he would take notice of. The result was that

though he won a war against Edom he lost one against
Israel. Until Jehoash died nine years later Amaziah
appears to have been his prisoner in the north, and when
at that point he returned to the south he found himself
cordially disliked. It was his fault, after all, that northern
troops had wrought such havoc in Jerusalem. Though he
was nominally king for the remaining fifteen years of his
life, he was dogged by conspiracy, and at some stage left
his capital to take refuge in Lachish, on the borders of
Philistia. Uzziah, though by now in the prime of life and
an experienced ruler, could not protect him, and he was
in the end assassinated, as his father Joash had been. The
thistle was finally crushed.

The cedar meanwhile flourished mightily. For the
greater part of Jehoash's reign his son had shared
the government of Israel with him, and now ruled as
Jeroboam II. The western campaigns of the Assyrian
kings had been designed to frighten and plunder the
Mediterranean states rather than to enlarge Assyria's
frontiers; they were raids, not invasions, though certainly
raids on the grand scale. Even these were now a thing of
the past, as preoccupations elsewhere kept the successors
of Adad-nirari busy. It was Israel that was able to expand,
till to north and east Jeroboam's rule stretched practically
as far as David's and Solomon's had. Everything came
together – power, influence, wealth, fame, and remarkable
ability – to make his years another golden age for Israel,
almost to be compared with that of its two greatest kings.

To crown it all, Jeroboam could claim that a prophet
had foretold these imperial splendours. No, really – a
genuine prophet of Yahweh, and one whose name would
resound down the ages, although in a rather different
connection: Jonah the son of Amittai. Jehoash had
basked (when it suited him) in the reflected glory of the
great Elisha. How encouraging for Jeroboam likewise to

think that Yahweh must be on his side!
Maybe. Or then again, maybe not.

XIV

'LONG TO REIGN OVER US'

For forty-one years Jeroboam II reigned over the northern kingdom, considerably longer than any other of its rulers. Such reigns were more common in the south; David and Solomon in the tenth century, Asa in the ninth, Uzziah in the eighth, and Manasseh in the seventh, each occupied the throne of Judah for forty years or more.

The figures can be misleading. Jeroboam's forty-one is to be counted not from the year of his father's death, but from the time his father made him co-regent, eleven years earlier. This is the Bible historians' regular practice. Because every co-regency meant the overlapping of two reigns, you cannot simply add the numbers end to end without making a hopeless muddle of the dating.

Uzziah's fifty-two, as well as being almost the longest of all the reigns of the Hebrew kings, is also in this respect the most complicated. The grandson of Joash, he was eleven when his grandfather was murdered, sixteen when his father was taken captive to Samaria and his own 'reign' began, twenty-five when Amaziah returned and a rather unsatisfactory co-regency was set up, and forty when on Amaziah's death he became sole king. At fifty-seven he made his son Jotham co-regent. It may have been at sixty-three that for reasons we shall presently discover he had to resign from public life, and for his remaining years till his death at sixty-seven he was an ex-king.

Whatever Uzziah's official title might be at any particular stage, his career was obviously keeping pace with Jeroboam's. No longer were odious comparisons made between the mighty cedar and the puny thistle. It must have seemed to the international community that the people of both kingdoms were very fortunate in their two monarchs, and presumably prayed regularly that Yahweh would continue to 'send them victorious, happy and glorious,' as well as causing them 'long to reign over us.'

Victorious they certainly were. While Israel was driving out the Arameans from the territories they had overrun to its north and east, Judah set about regaining lost lands to the south and west. Uzziah was in his element. He seems to have inherited something of David's military genius. Not for two hundred years had the kingdom been as well armed and as strongly defended as it was now, under his personal direction and supervision. His name means 'Yahweh is my strength', or 'Strong-in-the-Lord', and he lived up to it. He marched his armies against Philistia; the old unity of its Five Lords had crumbled, and they had become 'little kings' on the Canaanite model; Uzziah picked off their cities one by one, and planted new settlements of his own people among them. Ammon paid him tribute. He recaptured the last southern outpost of Edom. Even in Egypt he was famous.

Very unlike Uzziah in this respect was an equally long-serving, much more recent monarch, England's George III. The forces he sent abroad on their American campaign came home well and truly defeated. But in another respect the two rulers were alike. Uzziah would have appreciated the English king's nickname 'Farmer George'. A close interest in agriculture was something they had in common. The Bible remarks on Uzziah's numerous flocks and herds, farms and vineyards; 'he loved the soil', says the Chronicler. If he inherited his warlike gene from David, this side of him harks back to the arts of peace and the interest in the world of nature that were so characteristic of Solomon.

So, we may say, a happy and glorious reign for Judah; and one for Israel too, after its own fashion, if by happiness we mean prosperity. Both kingdoms saw something of the age of David and Solomon revived in this Indian summer they were enjoying. It was due not simply to armies that kept the peace and farmers who supplied the markets, but also to the fact that once again the Hebrew kingdoms, sitting astride the great trade routes of the Middle East, were profiting enormously from the free flow of commerce. Of the many achievements of Uzziah listed in 2 Chronicles, 2 Kings highlights just one: once his father had died and he was no longer merely regent but king in his own right, he 'rebuilt Elath', we are told. The name may be familiar from maps of modern Israel. They show the country's frontiers converging like an arrowhead that points south and touches the tip of the Red Sea at the holiday resort of Eilat. Solomon had made this neighbourhood an industrial and commercial centre, with copper- and iron-works and a port for his sea-borne trading enterprises. It had been lost to Edom, briefly recaptured in the days of Jehoshaphat (it was the location of his Ezion Geber shipbuilding scheme), lost again, and left to decay. But the mention of its rebirth in 2 Kings 14:22, with all that that implies, puts in a nutshell the 'happy and glorious' state of the Hebrew kingdoms towards the middle of the eighth century.

It was to all appearances *shalom*, a prosperous peace of the kind that Solomon had established. In the years between, only Jehoshaphat's reign had looked anything like it. But appearances are deceptive. Though to outsiders both the sister kingdoms must have seemed equally flourishing, two very different processes were going on, and two very different men could have explained them to us.

The one in the south both lived and belonged there. He was a courtier, an influential friend of King Uzziah's; and apart from that we know practically nothing about him. The one in the north did not belong to the north; he was a peasant, and no friend at all of King Jeroboam's, and to him the Old Testament devotes an entire book. There were many contrasts between these two. Even the initials of their names appear at opposite ends of the English alphabet!

Amos, driven by the Spirit of Yahweh, had left someone else to look after his fig trees and his herd of cows, and had made his way into Jeroboam's territory. It was no great distance from Tekoa, his home town, a few miles the other side of Jerusalem; past the capital he went, and on across the border to Bethel, where one of the rival temples had been built in the days of the first Jeroboam. The last man of God to appear in those parts, Jonah, was much more widely travelled. He had set out in one direction, though unsuccessfully, to go all the way to Spain, and had then gone in the other direction all the way to Assyria. This man, who had previously foretold Israel's present success, was sent to be the prophet of Assyria's threatened downfall. Amos now brought a similar doom-laden message home to Israel too.

It did not sound like that when he began to preach. Everyone listened approvingly as he talked about the surrounding nations, Aram and Philistia and the rest, their sins and the divine punishments that had already begun to fall upon them. How true, and how just! But when the lash of his tongue fell also upon Judah, and finally upon Israel itself, that was a different matter. Surely in respect of the 'happy and glorious' rule of Jeroboam II this was neither true nor just. Not only were the nation's coffers full, so too (as we might have put it) were the churches; Israel was religious as well as rich.

Amos exposed the truth about both church and state. Israel's prosperity was simply a temporary side-effect of Yahweh's larger plan for the destinies of all the nations, and in no way a sign that he approved of this one. As for 'full churches', do you notice, said the prophet, how many in these fashionable congregations are wealthy people who have made their money by doing down their less fortunate fellow-citizens? What is the point of all this 'worship' if there is no godly living? This is a sick society, and death is at the door.

Zechariah was the unsung hero of the parallel prosperity in Judah. There are many Zechariahs in the Bible (we have already met one, though not by name; he was the prophet martyred in the reign of Joash), and this one's claim to fame is summed up in a single verse, 2 Chronicles 26:5. The Bible does not call him either a prophet or a priest; but he was clearly a man of insight and a trusted mentor and adviser, for he 'instructed Uzziah in the fear, or in the vision, of God'. Through all the days of their friendship Uzziah 'sought the Lord', and 'as long as he sought the Lord, God gave him success.' On this relationship, therefore, were based the godliness, wisdom, and strength of one of the greatest kings of David's line, and on those in turn were based the security and well-being of his people. The wealth and worship of Judah, unlike those of Israel, represented real *shalom*, and a living relationship with Yahweh.

For seventeen years in the middle of his long reign, between the death of his father Amaziah and his co-opting of his son Jotham, Uzziah ruled Judah alone. It was towards the end of that time that things in Israel began suddenly to go downhill. In our next chapter we shall arrive at the period during which in a manner of speaking the southern kingdom had three kings at once. That was still some years away when the northern kingdom found itself unexpectedly in the much more upsetting situation of being ruled by four kings successively within the space of a single year.

You can imagine the views of Jeroboam's loyal subjects on their monarch and his successes: 'Though we may wish him "long to reign over us", we don't of course expect him to do so indefinitely. On the other hand, when he does die we see no reason why the good times should not continue regardless.' Well, in 753 he did die; and a memory may have surfaced somewhere of a prophecy concerning the House of Jehu. That king had so thoroughly rooted out the Baal-religion that had infected Israel in Ahab's time that Yahweh had promised to reward his descendants with a notable future. The House of Omri, to which Ahab belonged, had spanned three generations; Jehu would be the first of a dynasty that would rule for five.

Jeroboam was the fourth of the line, and his son, the new king (yet another Zechariah), was the fifth. We know from Amos's preaching what Yahweh thought of the glittering reign of Jeroboam II. Contrary to popular belief, the fate of nations was in the hands of the Lord God of Israel, as of course it always is; and to Yahweh's mind there was no reason why the good times *should* continue. Once Zechariah was on the throne, the fifth generation had arrived; the promise had been kept, and without any further delay the House of Jehu too would be taught that sins have consequences. In contrast to his father's long reign, Zechariah's had lasted only six months before a man called Shallum conspired against him, killed him, took his crown, and brought Jehu's dynasty to an end.

Shallum's reign was even shorter. Within a month he too was the victim of a coup, and died at the hands of Menahem, the governor of Israel's former capital Tirzah, who saw himself as the founder of a new dynasty and was to enjoy ten years of power in Samaria.

A memorable earthquake shook Israel a couple of years after Amos had been preaching there. It underlined his solemn warnings, which more than once had used the language of earth tremors and collapsing buildings as a metaphor of God's anger. Uzziah saw around him the unshaken *shalom* of Judah, and must have watched with awe as in Israel, which had seemed so strong and rich and stable, kings fell like a row of ninepins.

XV

THE BEE BUZZES

We go back before Israel's 'year of the four kings' to see why the ninety-year rule of the House of Jehu came to such a sudden end, and what had made its kingdom so politically unstable and triggered the social earthquake that caused its downfall.

At one level it was a matter of economics. Israel was wealthier than at any time since Solomon, but the way its wealth was distributed was grossly unfair. In the prosperity of Solomon's reign everyone benefited; in that of Jeroboam II the rich grew richer while the poor grew poorer. Walking through a northern town in the early eighth century, you would find palaces at one end and slums at the other, instead of the classless society which the laws of Moses envisaged, and which had actually existed two hundred years earlier. For many in Israel the days of the second Jeroboam were very far from being a golden age, and there was much dangerous discontent.

Underlying this was a breakdown in the system of public justice. Judges could be bribed; money talked; the law could be swung in favour of those who could pay, while for those who could not, exorbitant fees and fines might drive them into penury, if not slavery.

At a deeper level still, religion was the issue. Unlike any other of the ancient gods, Israel's Lord taught his people to love their neighbours; yet the very folk who thronged the temples in Samaria and Dan and Bethel one day would go out the next day not to love but to fleece their neighbours. It was the hypocrisy of their so-called worship of Yahweh that incensed Amos, and drove him to denounce it publicly in the presence of their so-called high priest in Bethel.

Another prophet, Hosea, had added his voice to that of Amos, deploring the same evils, and the nation's unfaithfulness to its loving God. His hearers were aware of something of the troubles of his personal life, and he used the sorry state of his marriage as a picture of that broken relationship. We owe a good deal of what we know about the period to the fact that God's messengers to Israel at that time (three of them, when we include Jonah) were no longer simply preaching, but also having their prophecies written down. A fourth such voice, the greatest of all the 'writing prophets' (of whom there were several yet to come), was soon to be heard, this time in the southern kingdom. To Judah therefore we have now to return, to set the scene for the career of Isaiah.

Given the news from the north, of the rapid series of regime changes sparked off by the death of Jeroboam, Uzziah must have been concerned about the stability of his own kingdom in the south. Perhaps it was because of this that in 750, as Menahem strengthened his hold on the throne of Israel, Uzziah set up the next of Judah's co-regencies, giving his son Jotham the now-familiar role of 'associate king'.

Jotham was a good man, in fact almost the only one

of all the Hebrew kings with whom the biblical records find practically no fault. Not even of his father can this be said. For towards the end of Uzziah's long and glorious reign something went spectacularly wrong. Every king of the House of David played a leading part in the religious life of his nation, but however great their prestige that did not mean they could simply do as they pleased in this regard. The ancient laws laid down who did what in the ceremonies of the Jerusalem temple, and much of the ritual was the responsibility of the priests, and of no one else. Long afterwards, the New Testament would describe God's people in terms of the human body, which works when each part does what it is designed to do, and does not work when one part tries to do the job of another. On this fateful occasion Uzziah decided – it was the kind of self-importance that had led his father into the disastrous 'thistle-versus-cedar' war with Israel – that he would take over the priests' prerogative of offering incense in the temple. He knew well that it was not something that just anybody had a right to do, but then he was not just anybody; he was the king. He was also, as the apostle Paul would have told him, an ear wanting to be an eye, or a foot deciding to do the job of a hand. As Yahweh's chosen representative, he more than anyone ought to have known better.

The indignation of the high priest in Bethel at the preaching of Amos was as nothing compared with the reaction of his opposite number in Jerusalem to what Uzziah was doing. Azariah and his fellow-priests confronted the king, and rebuked him for his presumption. Far from being abashed, Uzziah in his turn became angry. As he did so, the priests' anger changed to horror. They became aware not just of his wrath but also of a physical mark on his forehead: a discoloured patch of skin that was the first sign of leprosy, or of some other disease with similar symptoms and equally dire effects.

As they saw the change on his face, he saw the change on theirs. What could they be staring at? In that moment the mortified king must have realized what had happened. Whatever the infection would be in modern terms, and whoever the sufferer might be, it demanded instant action. They hurried him out of the temple, says the Chronicler, indeed he himself hurried to get out, knowing only too well that this was a judgment from Yahweh; sin always has consequences. The temple was no place for a 'leper'. Nor was the palace, nor any public place. It was effectively the end of Uzziah's reign. For the remaining years of his life he was confined to a 'separate house', which may or may not have been a kind of isolation hospital, but which either way meant he would play no further part in the nation's affairs.

So Jotham came to the throne very much as Uzziah himself had done: the reigning king removed from the scene as a result of a foolish and arrogant act, but still living, and his son having to take over. Between 743 and 739 there may have been three 'kings' simultaneously in Judah; this odd state of affairs would be explained by Uzziah's having already made Jotham co-regent in 750, and then having fallen from grace in 743, so that at that point his son and grandson would each have moved one step up, so to speak – Jotham to become 'acting king', that is, regent, and Ahaz to be Jotham's co-regent, while Uzziah lived on in retirement till 739.

As that eventful life came to an end, it may well have been in the very place where Uzziah had four years earlier forfeited his calling to be a king, that the young Isaiah received his calling to be a prophet. 'In the year that King Uzziah died,' he wrote later, 'I saw the Lord sitting on a throne, and the train of his robe filled the temple.' It was a reminder, two thirds of the way through the story of the monarchy, that for all the shortcomings of even the best of Israel's kings the real ruler was still Yahweh, and that though he was the Invisible King, he would nonetheless make himself known to those with the eyes to see.

Isaiah's ministry was to span the next fifty years. Ahaz would be on the throne by the time the prophet's eye was shown the curious picture that provides the titles for this chapter and the next: Yahweh whistling for the Egyptian fly and the Assyrian bee (Isaiah 7:18). What exactly did this prophecy mean?

Egypt and Assyria were of course the superpowers of the Middle East in those days, and each might at one time or another threaten the peace of the region. The Hebrew prophets tended to describe such enemies as lions or leopards, bears or wolves; insects would be a comparable threat only if they attacked in huge swarms, as in the plagues of gnats and locusts at the time of the exodus. The prophecy speaks in the singular, however, and what was menacing about one fly, or a single bee? Perhaps the arrogance of the Hebrew kingdoms had grown as their size increased under Uzziah and Jeroboam II, and these foreign powers which had once frightened them now seemed negligible; it was easy enough to swat an insect. If so, they were soon to discover how wrong they were. Or perhaps Yahweh was saying that to him Assyria really was negligible – even one of the world's superpowers could be as easily disposed of as an irritating insect; but before he eventually swatted it, he intended guilty Israel to find that it had a lethal sting.

Since Isaiah was commissioned by Yahweh only in the year of Uzziah's death, and the bee prophecy came some years later, when Ahaz was king, no one before that time would have grasped quite what kind of damage Assyria might one day do, and how deadly an enemy it might become. But the bee was already buzzing. Of that the northern kingdom in particular was aware. More than a century before, during Ahab's reign, one Assyrian king had marched his armies towards the Mediterranean, to be confronted by the combined forces of the western nations at the battle of Qarqar. Twelve years later he had returned on a similar campaign, and this time Jehu had bought him off. Jehoahaz was on the throne when after a gap of nearly forty years another Assyrian invasion had actually done Israel a good turn by destroying the power of Aram, which had been for so long a thorn in its side. All these expeditions were out for gain and glory rather than empire-building, and neither Shalmaneser's nor Adad-nirari's achieved anything very permanent or extensive. But in 745 a king of a different stamp had come to the throne in Assyria. His name was Tiglath-pileser III, and his aim was solid and lasting power at home and conquest abroad.

Through these middle years of the eighth century the authors of the books of Kings and Chronicles focus first on the four kings who ruled Israel in quick succession, Jeroboam and Zechariah, Shallum and Menahem, and then on the overlapping of three royal generations in Judah, Uzziah and Jotham and Ahaz. But the prophecies of Isaiah have a wider view. They spell out the fact that Yahweh directs the affairs of all the nations, and under his direction (though quite unaware of it) the new Assyrian king was at work in the far-off Land of the Two Rivers, consolidating his kingdom, reorganizing the way it was run, and setting about its expansion, so that while some of his neighbours paid a heavy price for his 'protection', others found their territories actually annexed, and even had large numbers of their people deported to other parts of the growing empire, or drafted into its armed forces. Yes, Tiglath-pileser was very busy, and observers throughout the Middle East could hear the ominous buzzing. It would not be long before this bee would respond to Yahweh's summons, the 'whistle' of which Isaiah's prophecy speaks, and would fly westwards for Israel's moment of destiny.

XVI

THE BEE STINGS

In Judah, Uzziah the king still had two years to live, and Isaiah the prophet had not yet been called to Yahweh's service, let alone been given the prophecy about the fly and the bee, when Menahem of Israel died and passed his kingdom to his son Pekahiah.

Not for the first time, a northern king seems to have seen nothing odd about taking the crown by force, yet assuming that his son should then inherit it by right. Nor was it the first time that a son who had been given a crown in this way failed to hold on to it. Menahem had been dead for only a couple of years when Pekahiah was killed in yet another coup, so that yet another would-be dynasty crashed at the first fence. Confusingly, the killer's name was the same as his victim's, except that Pekah has lost the 'Yah' element (which, as is the way with Bible names, could say something about the man himself).

Confusing is probably the right word for the whole account of the kings who followed Jeroboam II in Samaria in the eighth century. Like the successors of the first

Jeroboam, two hundred years before, most of the half-dozen names are unfamiliar, and few of them are memorable; their dates are puzzling, their fates are generally unpleasant. It is easy to skim the surface of the story. But we need to look under the surface if we are not to miss the connections and lose the plot.

It helps if we focus on the three kings who for better or worse did make some sort of mark on their times. Roughly speaking, in the northern kingdom the 740s belonged to Menahem, the 730s to Pekah, and the 720s to Hoshea; and how each of them coped with the challenges of his particular decade had a great deal to do with the buzzing of the Assyrian bee, which was becoming ever louder.

It was in the latter part of Menahem's reign that Tiglath-pileser came to power. The news from Assyria spread fast across the nations of the Middle East: new king, new policies, new perils. When the Assyrian war machine next rolled into action it would not be simply with a view to taking a lot of plunder home and leaving a fearsome reputation behind. This time full-blown imperialism was the name of the game. If you resisted, you would be defeated and your country would be occupied and absorbed into the Assyrian empire. If on the other hand you made friends with the enemy, you would survive, but pay a big price for the privilege, and become a satellite of the Assyrian empire anyway.

Menahem opted for the second way. He could afford to, with the wealth that Israel had amassed during Jeroboam's reign. Many thousands of his subjects who had grown rich in those days now found themselves liable to a new tax. No doubt they reckoned, as their king did, that the outlay was worth it, considering the alternative, and the fearsome cruelties for which Assyria was notorious. If you can't beat them, join them.

Pekah took the opposite view. It was not only, perhaps

not even mainly, out of personal ambition or the lust for power that he had removed Pekahiah. He had no mind to sit by while the House of Menahem threw away Israelite independence. An alliance of western states had stopped the Assyrian juggernaut in its tracks at Qarqar a hundred years earlier, and he saw no reason why history should not repeat itself. During the easy years the Arameans had rebuilt their kingdom around its ancient capital Damascus, and Pekah's Israel might make common cause with them, and (he hoped) with others of the nations of Palestine, to resist the new Assyria.

He ruled the northern kingdom for the best part of the next decade. He was well able to do so. When 2 Kings 15 gives him a twenty-year 'reign' and calls him a 'captain' or 'chief officer', it is counting as if for a co-regency, and using a term better translated as 'lieutenant' or 'deputy'; he may well have been ruling part of Israel (perhaps Gilead, to judge from the posse he brought with him to deal with Pekahiah) for as long as Menahem had been on the throne.

Israel and Aram had been fighting each other, on and off, for many years. It was time to bury the hatchet. The kings of the two nations put their heads together and considered who else might be drawn into an anti-Assyrian alliance. An obvious possibility was Judah. It appears that while Uzziah was still in charge there he had already gathered some allies together to stand up against this enemy. The attempt had no great success, though Uzziah had at least survived it. By now Jotham had taken his place. In many ways he was very much his father's son. A strong, just, god-fearing man, he too invested heavily in the welfare and defence of his country. There were however differences between them. On the credit side, Jotham took warning from the fate that had befallen Uzziah, and was careful always 'to walk humbly with his God', to quote the words of the prophet Micah, whose ministry began during his reign. On the debit side, he was unable to persuade his people to do the same. The new generation was growing careless about the God who in Uzziah's day had made Judah so prosperous.

But Jotham's heart at any rate was true, and must have been much encouraged by the presence of a prophet of Yahweh right there in Jerusalem with him – not yet Micah, but Isaiah. The pair of them knew well that as it grew harder to ignore the buzzing of the bee, the safety of their kingdom lay neither in selling out to the Assyrians nor in making alliances against them, but in looking to Yahweh in trust and obedience. Jotham therefore turned a deaf ear to the siren voices from the north, with their invitation to throw in his lot with Pekah of Israel and Rezin, the Aramean king in Damascus.

Sadly, his days were already numbered, and it was his son Ahaz who had to face the next move of the anti-Assyrian alliance. If Pekah and Rezin were to face an Assyrian attack from the north-east, they did not want immediately behind them a neutral state that could easily become an Assyrian ally. Judah must be made to join them.

If we put together the accounts of the reign of Ahaz in the books of Kings, Chronicles, and Isaiah, the first thing that happened when he came to power was, it seems, a repeat of the proposal that his father had already rejected. As Pekah and Rezin had approached Jotham, so now they put pressure on Ahaz. He too did not want to be involved, and this time they mobilized an invasion force, with the aim of capturing Jerusalem, deposing him, and installing one Ben-Tabeel, an associate of Rezin's, as king of Judah in his place.

Reports began coming in of the confederate armies massing on the frontier, not all that far north of Jerusalem. The hills were swarming with troops. 'Swarming' – an ominous word, in view of the message from Yahweh that was about to be passed on to Ahaz. We can picture the king emerging from the city by the Water Gate on its eastern side, with a group of advisers, to inspect the aqueduct that brought its essential water supply in from the Gihon spring, and to discuss how to protect this conduit in case of a siege. There to meet him came Isaiah, with the first of a cluster of prophecies that would expose him for what he was.

The two young men come face to face. The prophet has brought with him his little son, and introduces him to the king: Shear-Jashub, 'Remnant Returning' – that in itself must have a meaning, which may dawn on Ahaz in due course. 'Be careful; be calm,' says the Lord through his messenger, much like advice to a nervous landsman in a rocking boat, 'Mind you keep still'; don't be afraid of Pekah and Rezin, a couple of firebrands certainly, but already almost burnt out. You should be much more concerned, Ahaz, about Tiglath-pileser. Rather like the Philistine ranks falling back, three hundred years ago, when Goliath the giant stepped forth, this swarm of invaders will shrink into insignificance when I call the bee from Assyria. But whoever the enemy may be, *put your trust in me.*

Whether or not the king understood all this mix of metaphors (and there are a good many more in Isaiah 7 – 11), he got the main point, and decided to ignore it. War had already broken out, and it seemed to him that the swarms were going to destroy Judah. And indeed, in the event many of its people were captured, many were killed, Jerusalem was besieged (though not taken), and other old enemies, Philistines and Edomites, joined the coalition. Ahaz, ringed with foes, and unwilling to 'keep still' and trust Yahweh, panicked and appealed for help to Tiglath-pileser.

Ironically, therefore, the voice by which Yahweh summoned the bee was that of Ahaz himself. The Assyrians duly came, and in three campaigns drove down the western coast as far as the Egyptian border, overran Gilead to the east, and in the centre occupied the northern part of the northern kingdom. These would all become provinces of their empire; in a prophecy that looks forward to a different kind of conquest in the time of Jesus, Isaiah 9:1 calls them 'the way of the sea', 'the far side of Jordan', and 'Galilee of the nations'. Clinging to what was left of his kingdom, Pekah was murdered by a pro-Assyrian group, and his throne was seized by its leader, Hoshea. So began the reign of the last king of Israel – a vassal of Tiglath-pileser, of course, just as Ahaz now was, thanks to his ill-judged appeal for Assyrian protection.

Aram did not escape. Damascus was captured, Rezin, like Pekah, was killed, and his kingdom was turned into four more Assyrian provinces. Ahaz, with other rulers who had kept their crowns by siding with Tiglath-pileser, was called to its capital to abase himself in homage to the Great King.

Did he return to Jerusalem suitably humbled? Not a bit of it. Not one of his forefathers on the throne of Judah had cared as little as he did about the historic faith of Yahweh. He had allowed in, and encouraged, any amount of pagan religion alongside it: anything to hedge his bets, to keep his increasingly wayward people united, and (incidentally) to suit his own depraved tastes. Now, to crown it all, he came back eager to reorganize Yahweh's temple in Jerusalem so as to accommodate the latest blasphemies he had seen, when amid awe-inspiring Assyrian ceremonies he had bowed before his new overlord in Damascus.

In 2 Kings he and Hoshea are presented as another pair of mirror images. Ahaz was worse than any of his predecessors, Hoshea was not quite so bad as any of his. In what way he was an improvement we are not told; whatever it was, it could not delay the end of the northern kingdom. Hearing that Tiglath-pileser had died, he foolishly opened secret negotiations for an alliance with Egypt, and was bold enough to stop payment of his regular tribute to Assyria. The results were disastrous. He was arrested and imprisoned on the orders of the new king, Shalmaneser V, who sent an army to besiege Samaria. It took the rest of Shalmaneser's brief reign to bring the once-great capital to its knees; it fell in 722 after a three-year siege, and his successor Sargon II completed the job by deporting Hoshea's subjects in their thousands to the far corners of the empire, and replacing them with an assortment of deportees brought in from other conquered lands.

XVII

ONE WHO LISTENED

Yahweh has never left his people without some sort of witness to the kind of God he is. In New Testament times one of his most famous spokesmen, the apostle Paul, would go so far as to say that anyone anywhere can, in theory, learn something about 'his eternal power and deity' from the created world around us and the way it works; though he also made it clear that it was to Israel alone that the 'oracles of God' had been spelt out clearly. Every Israelite generation could learn from Moses and other great prophets of the past, whose teaching never dated. In addition, many of God's people, especially in the days of the kings, had the privilege of actually hearing a prophet speak. Amos had been sent from Judah to Israel in the prosperous days of the early eighth century, with a message of stern warning. Hosea belonged there in the north, and lamented his country's increasing wickedness. Micah, like Amos before him, was a southerner who spoke to the northern kingdom, while there still was a northern kingdom to be spoken to, but he was most burdened by the fact that Judah seemed to be on the same downward path. Again like Amos, he was a countryman; his home in Moresheth lay some distance south-west of Jerusalem, where the hills fall away towards Philistia and the sea. Isaiah, in contrast, was a man of the city, rubbing shoulders with the movers and shakers of his day. As the threat from Assyria grew and the good times came to an end, he had wise counsel for those whose hands were on the levers of power. All of these men brought vivid, hard-hitting messages from God for the days in which they lived. How often it must have seemed to them that their words were falling on deaf ears!

Of all the kings of the line of David so far, Ahaz was the deafest. We have already seen him refusing to hear Yahweh's warning, through Isaiah, that his safety lay neither in joining an anti-Assyrian alliance nor in appealing to Assyria for help against it, but in learning wholeheartedly to trust and obey the Lord. He was the son and grandson of godly kings; both Jotham and Uzziah, like others before them, had grown famously strong by just such a policy. But would he listen? No, he would not. He turned instead both to foreign armies and to foreign gods. In answer to his cry for help the Assyrians came, and as the Bible record states bluntly, they brought nothing but trouble. In fact 'they were the ruin of him and of all Israel', not only of the northern kingdom first under Pekah and then under Hoshea, but eventually of his own southern kingdom also. For though of the remaining eight kings of Judah two would go down in history as outstanding men of God, even they could only stave off the evil day temporarily. Judah and the Davidic monarchy would never henceforward be free from entanglement with the power politics of the Middle East, and had little more than a century to go before they were destroyed by it.

To the day of his death Ahaz followed the same wrong-headed agenda, and shut his ears to wise counsel. Hezekiah, succeeding him in 715, had very different ideas.

For the eighth-century prophets, so accustomed to not being listened to, the open ear of the new king must have been a refreshing change. In fact he was already listening to a voice from the past, that of a man seldom thought of as a prophet (though the New Testament says he was), namely the great king David. Through his teens and early twenties, as his father's co-regent, Hezekiah had watched Ahaz behaving like another Saul, a 'how not to be' king. Now that the throne was his, he would model his reign on that of Saul's successor, and try to be another David, 'a man after God's own heart'.

Learning from David's example, he was determined that Yahweh the God of Israel should once more take his rightful place at the centre of the nation's life. Not in 250 years had the people of God seen anything like the reformation that followed. All over the country, everything that had been allowed to infect or dilute or pervert their historic faith was identified and dealt with, from the latest poisonous innovations that Ahaz had sponsored to the longest-established and most deeply ingrained blots on the religious landscape. Even the bronze snake that Moses had made centuries before, in its time a wonderful symbol of Yahweh's love and goodness, was being worshipped as if it were an idol, so out it had to go.

The Jerusalem temple, which had suffered so much at the hands of Ahaz, was cleared and repaired, re-opened and re-staffed, and finally re-dedicated in a grand ceremony like the one with which Solomon had opened it originally. There followed an even grander event, a celebration of the Passover to which Hezekiah invited all true Israelites. It was still no more difficult to cross frontiers than it had been for most of Old Testament history; his messengers went all over the Assyrian provinces that had so recently been an Israelite kingdom, and though they had a mixed response from what was now a very mixed population, some of those who were left of the northern tribes did accept the invitation and were able to get to Jerusalem without hindrance.

That unforgettable Passover marked the beginning of a reign that would bring Judah a new prosperity, new military successes, and for Hezekiah a fame scarcely less than that of David and Solomon. His years were more truly a second golden age than even the reigns of Uzziah and Jeroboam II had been fifty years earlier.

And all this began to happen under the very noses of the Assyrians. So far as they were concerned, Judah was now one of their satellite states, and provided it kept in step and paid its tribute money regularly, its internal affairs were its own business. Hezekiah of course was doing his best to keep in step with a different drum. It was not always easy, and like David he was only human. Two events halfway through his twenty-nine years on the throne highlight first his strength and then his weakness.

At the age of about forty he fell seriously ill. The records mention simply a boil, or ulcer, but that was only the outward symptom of something much worse. He knew, and Isaiah came and confirmed, that in the prime of life he was facing death. Deeply distressed, he turned to Yahweh in prayer (in that long-practised trust lay his strength), and Isaiah, who had just left him, returned with a new message: God would not only heal him, but also give him another fifteen years to live, and moreover rescue both him and his city from the power of Assyria. For at some stage his loyalty as a vassal of the Assyrian kings had become suspect, and Judah was one of the states targeted by the latest of these kings, Sennacherib, when unrest along the Mediterranean seaboard brought him westwards to whip the rebels into line.

Sennacherib had already had to deal with a similar situation elsewhere in his empire. A former king of Babylon (what is now southern Iraq), by name Merodach-baladan, had himself become a vassal of Assyria some years earlier, but took advantage of the change of regime when Sennacherib came to the throne in 705 to set about regaining Babylon's independence. News of miracles surrounding Hezekiah's cure had reached him, and on the pretext of an interest in these events he sent envoys to Jerusalem to find out whether the king of Judah was willing and able to join yet another anti-Assyrian alliance. Flattered by the proposal, Hezekiah perhaps took it that this was how Yahweh intended finally to break the Assyrian yoke, and entered into frank and free discussions with the Babylonian envoys about the resources he might be able to bring to the enterprise.

The faithful Isaiah appeared as soon as the visitors had left, with another word from Yahweh. The God of Israel needed no help from anyone, whether the western states with possible support from Egypt, or Merodach-baladan and his Babylonians, to preserve his own people and deal with the Assyrian menace. He would not 'give his glory to another,' and Hezekiah should have known that. His response to the envoys ought to have been, 'Thank you, but no thank you.'

But he found it hard to work out quite what was meant by trust in Yahweh. Should he do nothing? Or should he do something, and if so, what? He was confident enough, it seems, to stop paying the annual tribute to Assyria, yet not confident enough to resist the idea of an anti-Assyrian alliance that would bind him to Tyre and Egypt and some of the Philistine city-states. This was the western conspiracy against which Sennacherib marched once he had dealt with the revolt in Babylonia.

Clearly however it was not Yahweh's intention to prevent the Assyrian armies crossing Judah's frontier or attacking and destroying Judah's towns. Hoping to avert an assault on his capital, Hezekiah sent the Assyrian king first an apology for not having paid tribute recently, and then a massive over-payment to make up for this offence. But being aware that Sennacherib might turn up all the same, Hezekiah also set about strengthening the defences of Jerusalem, ensuring a good store of weaponry, and protecting the city's water supply by having a tunnel cut from the Gihon spring outside the walls to a reservoir inside them (a famous feat of ancient engineering which can be explored to this day). None of this concern with walls and weapons and water was wrong in itself; but what had given rise to it was an invasion which might never have happened if Hezekiah had not gone against Isaiah's advice and aligned himself with Egypt and Co.

Sennacherib's main force had been dealing first with the Philistine city of Ekron and then with an Egyptian army that was coming to its aid. Crossing into the territory of Judah, he was now besieging the town of Lachish. Having troops enough and to spare, he sent a sufficiently large detachment of them to Jerusalem with three high-ranking officers as his spokesmen to frighten the besieged citizens into surrender. Frightened they were, but this time Hezekiah listened to Isaiah, and though the situation was of his own making, he was comforted to hear from Yahweh that the enemy's threats might safely be ignored.

Nonplussed at receiving no response, the Assyrian envoys went back to Sennacherib, leaving their army encamped around Jerusalem. Their king had captured and destroyed Lachish, and was on his way towards the capital. He sent another message demanding its surrender. Again Hezekiah turned to Yahweh, and again the response through the mouth of Isaiah brought him solid encouragement. In the memorable words of Lord Byron's poem, repeatedly in the later eighth century 'the Assyrian came down like a wolf on the fold', and for years every nation in the Middle East had known about the terror and suffering that regularly ensued. But this time – it was 701 – something different happened. The arrogant messengers of Sennacherib had fully expected that Israelite resistance would crumble at their threats; but another messenger, the supernatural 'messenger of Yahweh', says the Bible, marched through the Assyrian camp that night, striking down officers and other ranks alike, apparently by some sudden plague. In every Israelite home at the next Passover-time there would be a new depth to the reciting of the old story of the last plague of Egypt, when the Lord's destroying angel had passed over the land and 'there was not a house where there was not one dead'.

Perhaps for a combination of reasons (though that must have been one obvious one), Sennacherib decided to cut his losses and make for home. Future generations need not know of his failure to conquer Hezekiah; his sculptors would record in imperishable stone, on the walls of his palace in Nineveh, the tremendous victory at Lachish. The humiliating events at Jerusalem would soon be forgotten.

XVIII

DARK DAYS

The turn of the century, following Sennacherib's departure from Jerusalem in 701, was a turning point also in the life of Hezekiah.

From the start, it had been his aim to repair the damage his father had caused, once he was in a position to do so. As soon as Ahaz died, therefore, he had set about the reforms outlined in our last chapter, with the object of bringing Yahweh back into the centre of the life of his people. What was more, he had hoped that the first Passover of his reign might reunite the divided nation, which was why invitations to it had been sent across the frontier into what had so recently been the realm of the northern kings. After the campaigns of the 720s, in which the Assyrians had conquered Samaria, the usual droves of migrants were shunted to and fro across the empire, displaced from one country and relocated in another. This regular feature of Assyrian policy meant that not many Israelites were left there in the north; and of those that were, not many were interested in Hezekiah's proposal – only a remnant of a remnant. All the same, a fair number did accept.

So it had been a very special occasion. We today might describe that Passover as a 'national service of remembrance'. Like every Passover, it was a remembrance, a reminder of Israel's liberation from Egypt in the time of Moses. On the other hand, unlike any other Passover since the reign of Solomon it was national; there was at any rate a possibility of its bringing together representatives of all the twelve tribes. And it was service: not simply *a* service, a religious event, but a king and his people re-dedicating themselves to serve their God, 'not only with their lips, but in their lives'. 'Serve' is the word used throughout the Bible for one's relationship to one's God. And more than that, all who truly served the God of Israel would want to bracket another word with it. So reliable and loving was Yahweh, who could help but love him in return?

For the first half of his reign, then, Hezekiah both served and loved the God whom his father Ahaz had despised. At the halfway point (he was one of the few Bible people to be told how long he had yet to live!) he was taught another lesson, one that he probably thought he knew, but that needed to be brought into focus for him. A surprising statement of Yahweh's was going to be spoken through his friend the prophet Isaiah: 'There is no God but me; I make light, I create darkness, I make prosperity, I create calamity.' It was neither by chance nor by accident that Hezekiah had been stricken with a seemingly terminal disease, tempted to join a Babylonian conspiracy, and threatened by an Assyrian invasion. The God of Israel was behind all this. And there was something more to it than Yahweh's simply allowing unpleasant things to happen, and adapting his plans accordingly. He had intentions for his servant's long-term welfare which would not have worked out if Hezekiah had not experienced a 'calamity' or two. This son of David had long since learned how to serve and how to love. It took him longer to learn how to trust.

He took his revered ancestor David as his model even to the extent of composing a psalm, which is recorded in Isaiah 38. It was prompted by his illness and miraculous cure, but it reflects all the hard experiences of those middle years. He learned through them that it was his *shalom*, his welfare, that was Yahweh's purpose throughout; that is what the psalm celebrates. Little by little he grasped that nothing is outside the Lord's control, and that everything turns out in the end to have a loving purpose. The Bible histories record how in the remaining fifteen years that had been promised to him 'none of the kings of Judah trusted in Yahweh the God of Israel as he did', and how as a result 'he prospered in everything he undertook' and had 'very great riches and honour'.

So although the Assyrians had had their own objectives in the campaign of 701, there was as always a deeper plan in the mind of Yahweh of which their pagan kings knew nothing. Hezekiah's whole life was lived under the shadow of Assyrian aggression, yet the biblical histories see his reign as another golden age like that of David and Solomon, a testimony before the watching world to the greatness of Israel's God. In the words of Psalm 91, a thousand fell at his side and ten thousand at his right hand, but he and his kingdom were preserved even through the ultimate tests of a life-threatening illness and an invasion that reached the very gates of Jerusalem, and they emerged to another fifteen years of blessing, as everyone up and down the Mediterranean coast could see.

How strange and how sad, therefore, that his own son Manasseh could not see it. In the sharpest possible contrast to Hezekiah, the father being arguably the best of all the kings of Judah and the son undoubtedly the worst, Manasseh is a tragic figure as well as a wicked one. As an impressionable child he had witnessed the extraordinary events of those middle years; how could he have failed to grasp the reality of both the great power of evil and the even greater power of the true God?

But somehow the lesson was lost on him. At the age of twelve he was made co-regent with his father, and ten years later, when Hezekiah died in 686, he became king; and for most of his adult life Assyria's power, not Yahweh's, was for him the overwhelming reality.

His way of confronting it centred on religion rather than politics or armaments. He did have the overriding political aim of keeping his head down and not offending any of the line of powerful kings who ruled the empire from Nineveh, Sennacherib and Esarhaddon and Asshurbanipal. But to his mind the religious reforms of his father's reign seemed dangerously like a declaration of independence and a challenge to Assyria. The safe policy was to play down the exclusive claims of Israel's God, and not to look too different from everyone else.

It is ironic that a man with not an ounce of spirituality in him should go down in history as a religious fanatic. Then as now the Middle East was a multi-cultural society, and even within Judah the various faiths jostled for a place. The religion of Yahweh had tradition, the illustrious memory of Hezekiah, and the influence of the aged Isaiah to back it. The religion of Asshur had to be at least respected if you were to keep on the right side of the Assyrian king in Nineveh. The religion of the Baal-gods of old Canaan was never far below the surface, as popular as ever when it was allowed to flourish; the Baals could always be persuaded, or bribed, to do what you wanted, unlike Yahweh who always expected you to do what he wanted; the worship of that sort of god easily tipped over into mere magic.

This last was Manasseh's choice. Whereas his father's reign had become a single-minded celebration of King Yahweh, his own became an equally single-minded pursuit of witchcraft and the occult, necromancy and superstition, and fierce persecution of all who disagreed with King Manasseh; and he 'filled Jerusalem from end to end with innocent blood.' To the faithful in Judah it must have seemed an unending nightmare. More than half of this longest of reigns was given over to a religious enterprise steeped in wickedness and cruelty.

Another of its ironies was that these doings, by which Manasseh believed he was preserving his kingdom, were the very things that had caused the downfall of the old Canaanite kingdoms when the Israelites first arrived in their country. He was putting Judah at risk, not safeguarding it. Yet the majority of his people did not see things that way. Though there were many who suffered, there were more who were quite prepared to abandon Hezekiah's faith, to go with the changing wind, and to veer round and line up with Manasseh's policies. In Yahweh's eyes Judah as a nation was reaching the point of no return. The die was cast; the kingdom's fate was sealed, and even if Manasseh were to have a change of heart it would not now make any difference. The people had made their own decision.

Unexpectedly, his heart did change. The account in Kings is concerned only with the long-term effect of his wickedness, namely the downfall of the Hebrew monarchy. Since no later doings of his could now prevent that, the author of Kings saw no point in recording them. Even so, Manasseh might yet be rescued from himself, and learn a personal lesson from the immediate consequences of his actions; hence the fuller account in Chronicles. As his sins multiplied, so did Yahweh's warnings. Legend has it that the veteran Isaiah was silenced in the great persecution, but a succession of other prophets followed him, and when the king proved deaf to them all, there came an accusation and a summons that not even he could ignore.

It was fifty years since Hezekiah and Merodach-baladan

had met for secret talks about the possibility of a united stand against the power of Assyria, and now at the end of the 650s, after many such alarms elsewhere, Assyrian intelligence suspected fresh conspiracy in Jerusalem, and found it was only too real in Babylon, where open revolt broke out. Asshurbanipal, who had ruled the empire since 669, quelled the revolt, and sent an armed force to arrest Manasseh and take him from one city to the other for 'investigation'.

So great was Manasseh's fear of the king of Assyria, and of what might await him when he arrived in Babylon (the Chronicler's phrase 'taken with hooks' may mean something as nasty as it sounds), that he rediscovered at last his fear of the God of Israel. The scales fell from his eyes. He turned back to Yahweh and begged him for mercy, repented of his manifold sins, found himself to his huge relief cleared of suspicion after all and sent home to Judah in one piece, and spent the rest of his reign trying to undo the harm he had done.

It was all too late. The ship of state was a cumbersome vessel, and Manasseh's earlier efforts to steer it the way he wanted had been so thorough and so successful that now not even he, reformed character though he was, could bring it back on to the right course.

Thanks to those previous policies, his son Amon had been born into a nation whose traditional beliefs had gone right out of fashion. It is scarcely surprising that as a young man Amon did not take kindly to Manasseh's sudden change of mind and the re-imposing of old-fashioned strait-laced religion. For almost ten years he and his generation must have chafed against his father's attempts at reform. Then in 642 Manasseh died, and the crown was his.

At once Judah began to move again towards its doom. People who had hoped that the days of Hezekiah might be returning found themselves pitched instead into a repeat of the early days of Manasseh. With the accession of Amon the Baals were back in vogue, no sensible person took Yahweh seriously, and those who persisted in doing so were extremely unpopular. It must have seemed to such people that their God, the Light of Israel, was finally leaving his nation to its own devices. The bright day was done, and they were for the dark.

XIX

SPLENDID SUNSET

Suddenly, without warning, came yet another change. The faithful remnant in Israel, those who had most reason to dislike Amon, were also the least likely to take it on themselves to remove him. They would have accepted the teaching of Moses, that vengeance is Yahweh's responsibility. They would have understood the words of David: 'Saul is the Lord's anointed king; not even I dare harm him.' But in the case of Amon somebody else did dare. His servants, say the histories; we are not told their motives; but he had been ruling for only two years when he was assassinated in some kind of palace intrigue. If it was the throne his murderers wanted, their coup failed, for a number of Judah's leading citizens dealt out summary justice, executed them, and proclaimed Amon's little son Josiah king in his place.

The coronation was not unlike that of the sixteen-year-old Uzziah, when his father was taken hostage to Samaria. Josiah was half that age, and Joash had been younger still, when Israelite leaders concerned for the Davidic kingship saw to it that at such critical points in its history the family line was not broken. And there were still such people in Judah, people of faith and integrity, in spite of the spirit of the age that seemed so often to be destroying all that the kingdom stood for.

It must have been a group of this kind, driven underground by Manasseh's persecution, emerging again during his reforms, then suppressed once more by Amon, that now re-surfaced a second time and set up the reign of the new child-king. By the mid-seventh century the anti-Yahweh party too was reappearing regularly on the political scene, having twice been in power and being still popular when out of it. All the same, it was Yahweh's plan that Judah should for the moment be spared yet another spell of bad government. This was not so as to give his people one more chance to escape their doom (things had gone too far for that), but so as to give them one final taste of the rule of a godly king, a 'man after God's own heart', a true son of David.

More than most of the Hebrew kings, Josiah has the stages of his life clearly outlined in the Old Testament record. Born in the latter part of his grandfather's reign, in 648, he succeeded his father at the age of eight (640), 'began to seek the God of his father David' at sixteen (632), set about reforming Judah's religion at twenty (628) and was restoring the Jerusalem temple at twenty-six (622), and died in battle at thirty-nine (609). The histories tell us a lot about the events of 622, but considerably less about those of the other dates and of the spaces between.

These gaps are thought-provoking. Josiah was going to be one of Israel's great reformers, but we should be wrong to assume that his reign was from start to finish another golden age like Solomon's or Uzziah's or Hezekiah's. In the early years his guardians may have been politically supporters of the House of David, but the religious life of

Judah continued to be dominated by the false gods, and the priests who served them. As the New Testament would put it, Josiah was growing up 'in the midst of a crooked and perverse generation'. When the Bible tells us that in his mid-teens the historic faith of Israel became real to him, it sparks off a series of questions. How did that happen? And given that it did, why had it not happened earlier? Who were his teachers before the event, and who were his advisers after it? Then again, he had been on the throne for twelve years before he felt he knew what Yahweh wanted him to do, and had the courage to do it. For the pagan priesthood that still had great influence throughout the land, how unexpected was the revolution that began in 628, and was it sudden or gradual?

Whatever the answers to these questions, Josiah very likely saw his twentieth birthday as both his coming-of-age and the right time to embark on his real life's work, encouraged both by the situation in Judah and by that in the wider world.

At home, such respected leaders as the high priest Hilkiah, whom we shall meet presently, had no doubt acted as regents governing Judah during the years of his minority, much as Jehoiada had ruled the nation on behalf of the young Joash two centuries before. This then would be the point at which the young Josiah, after a kind of co-regency in his later teens, would become king in his own right.

On the international scene, unthinkable changes were about to take place, not unlike those that 2,600 years later would sweep across another vast empire immediately to the north of Assyria's. Who could have imagined in the mid-twentieth century A.D. the suddenness with which the Soviet Union would collapse? Just as unassailable seemed the power that Asshurbanipal inherited from his father Esarhaddon in 669 B.C. What is now northern Iraq was his empire's heartland; southern Iraq (Babylonia) was to be governed by his brother; his control extended eastwards across Iran and north-westwards across Syria and well into Turkey, and south-westwards he completed his father's conquest of the old enemy Egypt by sacking the city of Thebes, 400 miles up the Nile Valley. It was the largest empire the world had ever seen. It was also highly civilised, with trade and wealth, art and literature and great public works. But it was cruel, and it was hated; and when to the plotting of its subject nations was added the massing of migrating barbarians round its frontiers, not even the genius of Asshurbanipal would have been able to hold it together.

It was still more or less intact when he died, round about the time of Josiah's coming-of-age. But already he had lost control of Egypt; perhaps Manasseh was released after his visit to Babylon in order to build up Judah as a loyal outpost of the empire, or at least a buffer state, against the possibility of a renewed Egyptian threat. Then quite suddenly the whole unwieldy structure began to fall to pieces. The province of Babylon was turned into an independent kingdom by its governor Nabopolassar. In the eastern mountains (today's Iran) the Medes under Cyaxares made a similar bid for independence. Between them these two attacked and destroyed city after city – Asshur, Nineveh, Haran, you can trace the campaigns of the 610s across the map – with Asshur-uballit II, the last king of Assyria, falling back step by step before them, till at last, in 609 (a date to which we shall return), at Carchemish on the upper Euphrates he gave up the struggle, and Assyria was no more.

Two decades elapsed between the death of Asshurbanipal and the death of his empire. They coincided, in the providence of God, with the time given to Josiah to achieve the task for which he had been chosen. In 628, while the rest of the nations of the Middle East were otherwise engaged, he saw his opportunity, and took it. The time was ripe for him to put into effect the plans he had been mulling over for the previous four years: not only did he have allies at home, but also now there would be no officious interference from outside.

Of those twenty years the unforgettable one was 622. He and his colleagues in government, and a great many other people besides, were in the midst of a major project, the complete restoration of the much neglected, frequently misused, temple in Jerusalem. Hilkiah the high priest, talking with Shaphan the 'scribe' (read Secretary of State – these two were among the highest officials in the land) about the funding of the repairs, added: 'By the way, look what I've just discovered.' It was a scroll: the two men, and the king when they went off post-haste to show him, found themselves listening to the words of Moses, in what we call the Book of Deuteronomy. This was of course a famous old document; everyone knew about it vaguely, but no one had paid attention to it for a long time, and this, perhaps the official copy, had been gathering dust in a forgotten corner in the temple for who knew how long.

A group gathered round and learned, ashen-faced, just how far their nation had strayed from these God-given standards, and what dire judgment might await them. Was Josiah's programme of reform still not radical enough? As always in the days of the kings it was through the law and the prophets that Yahweh's voice was regularly to be heard. The book of the law was once again before them; was there a prophet to explain and apply it?

There was. Not Nahum, who had foretold the downfall of Nineveh, or Zephaniah, who had warned Judah of a like fate unless it repented, though Josiah will have looked up to both of these men in his earlier years; not the great Jeremiah, who was only just beginning his long ministry; but a prophetess, Huldah, to whose house in Jerusalem the king's advisers promptly went.

Their fears were confirmed. Judah was indeed doomed, though the doom would not come in Josiah's time. At least the nation could be called to rally round its young king to make a formal renewal of its ancient covenant with Yahweh, and to celebrate a Passover that would also take them back in heart and mind to the evergreen truths of those earliest times. What occasions these were! The Passover outdid even Hezekiah's in magnificence. Together with Josiah's ongoing crusade to rid Israel of every trace of false religion, which took him to all parts of both kingdoms now that Assyria was in no position to stop him, these achievements set the seal on his greatness. 'Neither before him nor after him was there any king so wholeheartedly committed to the ways of Yahweh made known through Moses,' says the author of Kings. Yet not even this, he continues, could avert the fate that had been awaiting the nation since the days of Manasseh.

If there is one minus point in the story of Josiah it is his needless death in battle when he was not yet forty. The year was 609. Egypt, ruled by a dynasty set up by Asshurbanipal when he overran the country, had since regained its independence, but was ready to come to the aid of the last Assyrian king in trying to check the rapidly growing power of Babylon. Josiah on the other hand wanted to see the power of Assyria finally extinguished, and learning that Egyptian forces led by the new pharaoh Necho II were on their way to reinforce the Assyrian remnant at Carchemish, he set out to stop them. He should not have provoked the fateful clash at the pass of Megiddo; and he did not survive it.

But over against that foolish decision we ought to set a very big plus point that emerges from his story as a whole. For all his championing of the cause of Yahweh, for all his desire to revive the old faith of Israel, there are many hints that Israel itself was distinctly cool about the whole idea.

With Assyria's decline, circumstances seemed easier than they had been for some time; what was the point of all this fanaticism? The nation depicted in the early chapters of Jeremiah's book shows none of Josiah's enthusiasm for the things of God. He carried his reforms through regardless of its widespread indifference; and also regardless of the fact that in a sense they were pointless, and he knew it – Huldah had told him so. But he also knew what his calling and responsibilities were, and from that agenda he never wavered, whether or not his people were with him. His kingdom was doomed, whatever he might do. Yet still, heroically, he did it.

A splendid figure, then, surpassing all that had gone before him. But it was the splendour of a sunset. Night was about to fall.

XX

NIGHT FALLS

About the time that Asshurbanipal of Assyria died, leaving behind him the largest empire the world had yet seen, and Josiah of Judah took up the reins of government in his tiny kingdom, determined to make of it something that would be at any rate good, if not particularly great, Yahweh the God of all nations was bringing a new actor on to the scene. Unknown to these kings, the teenage son of a priestly family in the village of Anathoth, a little way out from Jerusalem and near Judah's northern border, was destined to become more famous and more influential than either of them.

Young Jeremiah may have had ideas about what he might become in later life, but being a prophet was not one of them. He was a sensitive soul, and was appalled to learn from Yahweh's very first message to him – we are not told how it came, but there was no mistaking what it was or where it came from – that yes, a prophet he was to be, and that he would regularly have to announce unpopular news, and be hated because of it.

He was never given a message for Josiah, though he shared with the youthful king, only three or four years his senior, a desire to give himself heart and soul to the service of Yahweh. They seem to have followed separate but parallel paths, Josiah trying to bring his people back to the true God and Jeremiah warning what would happen if they refused to be brought.

As we know, within twenty years of the start of this campaign the mighty Assyrian empire was no more, and Josiah too had perished. In spite of his reforms the heart of his nation was unchanged; you cannot make people good by Act of Parliament. But he had done what he had been called to do, and it dovetailed with Jeremiah's task. He had demonstrated that in spite of all the efforts of the godliest of kings, the kingdom was past saving.

He had had his supporters, and some of them were still respected figures in Jerusalem after his death, and did their best to protect Jeremiah through the hard times that were to follow. Unlike Jeremiah, who never married, Josiah had married early, and had four sons in quick succession. It seems that the first of them, Johanan, died young; but when their father was killed in battle with the Egyptians, it was the fourth of the young fellows, not the second, that these 'elder statesmen' decided would be most likely to follow in Josiah's footsteps.

Each of the last four kings of Judah was going to have a 'throne-name', rather like the sons of George V of England who each in turn inherited his crown in the 1930s, first David as Edward VIII and then Albert as George VI. Accordingly Shallum became Jehoahaz (both names had belonged earlier to northern kings, we recall), and was duly enthroned in Jerusalem.

But not for long. Though Necho of Egypt, who had brushed aside Josiah's challenge at Megiddo, could not save his Assyrian allies in their final confrontation with the Babylonian armies on the River Euphrates, he saw himself as Babylon's great rival in Middle Eastern politics as the seventh century drew to a close. He intended that all the lands on his side of the river should form a united 'western alliance', in effect an Egyptian empire. With that in mind, he could not afford to have another independently-minded king like Josiah in Jerusalem. As it turned out, Yahweh did not approve of Jehoahaz either, though for different reasons. Those who had chosen him as the new king must have been mortified to find that while he may have shared his father's politics, he certainly did not share his faith. Returning three months later from the summer's campaigning, Pharaoh Necho brought about what Yahweh intended to happen, and simply removed the unsatisfactory monarch, taking him to Egypt as a prisoner, and replacing him by the eldest of Josiah's surviving sons, Eliakim.

Out of the frying pan and into the fire. Eliakim became Jehoiakim, Judah became once more the openly faithless nation that Josiah had tried so hard to reform, and Jeremiah became the prophet of doom that he never wanted to be. The people decided that they could put up with the faith of Yahweh after all (Josiah having banned all the rest), provided they could wilfully misunderstand it to mean that as long as they looked after 'religion' Yahweh would look after them, however godless their thinking, however immoral their lives. The king decided that like cynical politicians everywhere he could double the taxes so as to fund both the bills that had to be paid, such as the heavy tribute required by his Egyptian overlord, and the luxuries he wanted for himself, such as a brand new palace five miles west of Jerusalem. Jeremiah spoke out against all this, and made himself very unpopular, though for the time being he still had friends in high places. Three generations of the family of Shaphan, Josiah's secretary, repeatedly championed his cause and saved him from those who wished him ill.

The years 605-604 were momentous ones on several counts. Once again at Carchemish on the upper Euphrates two armies met, and the king of Egypt found he was no match for the crown prince of Babylon, newly appointed commander-in-chief of the Babylonian forces. This was the famous Nebuchadnezzar. Necho was soundly defeated, and chased all the way home, leaving his recently-acquired territories to a new overlord. Nebuchadnezzar was recalled to Babylon almost at once to be crowned king, his ailing father having died, but would soon be back to receive homage – and plunder and hostages – from these subject nations in the west. (Judah's contribution on this occasion included Daniel and his friends.)

Jehoiakim was exchanging one political master for another, but there was no getting rid of Jeremiah. The two men's mutual contempt was soon to be made very public. Yahweh had been giving his prophet a new kind of message: that his prophecies to date should be put in book form. In those times of course this meant a hand-written scroll, and a loyal friend, Baruch, had taken on the job of preparing it at Jeremiah's dictation.

These words from Yahweh were next heard in the temple, read out by Baruch (Jeremiah was barred from the place). A big assembly had been called, perhaps because of the looming political crisis as the Babylonians took over the kingdoms of Palestine. In the crowd was a grandson of Shaphan's, Micaiah, who instantly grasped the importance of what he heard, and ran to the government offices where Jehoiakim's cabinet, of which his father was a member, was in session. In consternation they heard Micaiah's report, then sent for Baruch to bring the scroll and read the actual words.

The nub of the matter was that Babylon was the 'foe from

the north' with whom Jeremiah had so often threatened Yahweh's rebellious people, and that the kingdom's doom was at hand. This was dynamite. The cabinet advised Baruch that for their own safety he and Jeremiah should go into hiding, while they went to tell the king what was happening.

It was December of 604, and a fire was lit in the royal apartments. The prophecy was reported to Jehoiakim, which was the sixth time it had been heard, and then he demanded to see the manuscript and hear it read out, which was the seventh. What happened next is one of the most shocking incidents in Old Testament history. The king took a pen-knife, cut off each section of the scroll as it was read, and threw it into the fire. So this son of David, the latest in the line of Yahweh's chosen kings, had the impertinence to dismiss a seven-times-repeated warning from his real Overlord, the Invisible King. Some of those present protested at this treatment of the words of the living God by one who more than most should have known better, but they were ignored; the rest were as unmoved as the king himself.

No thunderbolt fell from heaven. For the time being Jehoiakim kept his throne. He was Nebuchadnezzar's vassal for three more years, then changed sides when in 601 Egypt seemed to be in the ascendant again. But the Babylonians returned in force in 598, and by winter were besieging Jerusalem. The blaspheming king at last died the death he deserved, and his eighteen-year-old son Jehoiachin, his kingdom reduced to the square mile of its capital city, reigned over it for just three months, till it fell to Nebuchadnezzar's troops.

The kind of deportation that had taken Daniel to Babylon seven years earlier was now repeated on the grand scale. This time Ezekiel, another prophet-to-be, was among the deportees, as were the new king, most of the royal family, and many eminent or able or pro-Egyptian citizens. Jehoiachin was replaced by his uncle Zedekiah (two more throne-names; the last two kings of Judah, Josiah's grandson and then his only surviving son, were otherwise known as Jeconiah and Mattaniah).

Zedekiah, who was in any case a weak-willed individual, was thus left as a puppet-king with a second-rate team of advisers, which no longer included those who had previously stood up for Jeremiah. It was backed by so-called 'prophets', who since Josiah had reinstated Yahweh as the nation's official God now spoke in his name, and were all the more dangerous on that account. Whatever Jeremiah passed on as a true word from Yahweh they would simply contradict.

All Judah's leaders were against him. They believed that nothing was yet final, that the balance of power would continue to seesaw between Babylon and Egypt, that they could still play off one against the other and hope even to regain their independence one day. Jeremiah insisted, on the contrary, that the die was cast, that there was no more room for manoeuvre, that Babylon was Yahweh's chosen weapon to punish his people, and that paradoxically their only hope for the future lay in their accepting the fact.

And indeed after nine years of this sort of thing Nebuchadnezzar had had enough of it, and returned to besiege Jerusalem once again. Even then the end was not sudden. The eighteen-month siege was interrupted by news of a move by Egypt. Necho II's successor, Psamtik II, was a cautious ruler, but he had just been succeeded by a new pharaoh, Hophra, who was eager to stir up trouble in Palestine. The Babylonians' grip on the city was relaxed as they prepared for a threatened invasion; people in the capital were free to come and go, and no doubt took the opportunity to lay in extra provisions just in case, or even to move away altogether. The pro-Egyptians were vindicated,

Jeremiah was wrong again. But he wasn't. The threat from Hophra evaporated, Nebuchadnezzar's troops returned and this time remained, and the siege dragged on till the vain hopes of Zedekiah and his government evaporated also. On the very day, in the summer of 586, that supplies finally ran out and starvation stared the people of Jerusalem in the face, the besiegers broke through the northern walls and burst into the city. Zedekiah tried to escape under cover of night, but was overtaken on the road to Jericho. He was taken the 200 miles to Riblah in Syria, Nebuchadnezzar's base for his western campaigns, where he was blinded after being made to watch the execution of his sons, and then taken away in chains to die in obscurity somewhere in Babylonia. A month later, when Nebuchadnezzar's men came back to Jerusalem to carry out the methodical destruction of the entire city, everyone else of any consequence who was still living in the area was likewise deported to Babylon. Night had fallen on the Hebrew kingdoms.

XXI

THE INVISIBLE KINGDOM

The question was, where now was Yahweh's kingdom? The map of the Middle East, in the eleventh century a patchwork of colours, looked very different in the sixth century. Around the edges, there were still trackless deserts to the south; a network of city-states, which included the beginnings of Greece and Rome, fanned out westwards across the Mediterranean from Tyre; and new empires – Lydia, Media, Persia – had since arisen to north and east. But now, in 586, the map was dominated by just two great powers, Egypt and Babylon, with the latter much the larger of the two. Still a handful of the small nations of western Asia, like Ammon and Edom, clung to their independence, and it was from that short list that Judah had just been deleted.

So where was Yahweh's kingdom? To start with its historic place on the map, could it continue to exist in some shape or form in Palestine?

In Jerusalem, one of its few true representatives was Yahweh's prophet Jeremiah. Most of the patriotic party in Judah, the nationalists, hoping for help from Egypt but determined in any case to resist Babylon to the end, were now either dead or on their way into exile. It was the prophet and his faithful friends, regarded as traitors by the hawks in Zedekiah's government, who had survived.

Another prophet, Habakkuk, had had to come to terms with the fact that Nebuchadnezzar's armies (the Chaldeans, as he called them) were both a terrible foe who would inflict great suffering, destroy Judah, and in the end be punished for doing so, and also at the same time God's chosen means for disciplining his rebellious people, and to be accepted as such. Jeremiah knew all this, and was repeatedly driven to say the same sort of thing, though it was deemed disgracefully unpatriotic, and led to beatings, imprisonment, and attempts on his life. During the lull in the siege of Jerusalem, he had set out to walk to Anathoth to deal with some family business, but had been arrested by Zedekiah's soldiers on suspicion of defecting to the enemy. Thrown not just into prison but into an underground cistern (fortunately it had no water in it, only mud, though that was almost as bad), he was rescued by friends, with the connivance of the king, who always had a sneaking regard for him. But he was still under arrest when the city finally fell, and was freed by the Babylonians, who were aware that he had constantly advised Judah to accept their terms, and saw him as an ally.

The family of Shaphan, Josiah's secretary of state back in the 620s, had always supported him. It was one of them, Gedaliah by name, another grandson of Shaphan's, that Nebuchadnezzar appointed as governor over what was left of the Israelite nation.

I say Jeremiah and Gedaliah represented the kingless kingdom 'in Jerusalem', but in fact not even that now remained. A month after its capture Nebuchadnezzar had ordered the city to be cleared, looted, torched, and levelled.

It was uninhabitable. The ancient town of Mizpah, a few miles north, became Gedaliah's humble headquarters. The Promised Land had expanded to a considerable empire in the days of David and Solomon; could the tiny area to which it had now shrunk, without even a decent capital city, conceivably be the ongoing kingdom?

It was not long before that too was lost. An ex-army officer named Ishmael, fiercely anti-Babylonian and in league with the Ammonite king across the Jordan, assassinated Gedaliah, rounded up the people of Mizpah, and herded them off in the direction of Ammon. Along with the governor, the victims of this psychopath's killing spree had included, bizarrely, a company of Israelite pilgrims going to the ruined temple site in Jerusalem, but also, more significantly, the entire Babylonian garrison of the town. A fellow officer, Johanan, was keenly aware of how Babylon might react to such sniping at the edges of its empire. He chased after this latest sad procession of displaced persons, sent Ishmael packing, and then had to decide where they should all go now. Mizpah was out of the question. Once Gedaliah's death became known, Nebuchadnezzar's troops were bound to be back yet again with reprisals.

One place where the refugees would surely be safe was Egypt. Into the pharaoh's dominions they duly went; and you could argue, as they probably did argue, that the colony they established there was the remnant of Israel, all that was left of the kingdom. After all, they included on the one hand some surviving members of the royal house of David, and on the other hand the most eminent Israelite of the day, for they took Jeremiah to Egypt with them.

But they were wrong. The future did not lie with them, and the Egyptian project would prove to be a dead end. They had actually requested the prophet for a decision from Yahweh as to whether they should go there; after a ten-day wait (ever the reluctant spokesman, he would not dream of merely giving his own opinion), the answer came: No, against all their inclinations they should stay and entrust themselves to the hated Babylonians, they should not go to Egypt. So they went. They deliberately disobeyed an explicit word of God, although they had asked for it and had promised to act upon it. True Israelites indeed – truly incurable rebels.

If the kingdom did have a future, and it was neither in Judah nor in Egypt, might it be in Babylon, as Jeremiah had long insisted? An Israelite king still lived; not indeed the last one who had reigned in Jerusalem, for Zedekiah had been put to death in 586, but his nephew Jehoiachin, exiled eleven years earlier. In a kind of weird pre-echo of events in New Testament times, a king of the Jews, still only about thirty years of age, had been condemned by a pagan ruler to die in some Babylonian prison. Could there nonetheless be a new life ahead for him? And would there be a resurrected kingdom too?

Yes and no. The people of Yahweh had been a kingdom, a state ruled by a succession of monarchs starting with Saul and ending with Zedekiah, for about 450 years. By the end of that time the kingdom model had served its turn, and they had to begin to learn new ways of being God's own special nation. In another pre-echo of New Testament times they now found themselves scattered among the other nations, no longer marked out and bound together by frontiers drawn on a map, though still united in deeper, more important ways. Never again in their own particular area of the Middle East would they be ruled from Jerusalem by a descendant of David. The kingdom in that sense was finished and dead, though for a short time there would be an imitation of it, when a revived Jewish community centred on a rebuilt Jerusalem would be ruled, long afterwards, by a line of high priests calling themselves kings. Babylonians and Persians and Greeks would all have come and gone, and it would be to the Romans, half a millennium after the days of Jeremiah, that the last of these priest-kings would hand over his power.

But throughout that time the historic land of hills and rivers was still there, and the historic nation of flesh-and-blood people still survived. There would be more experiences, more lessons to learn, through the rest of those countdown years 'before Christ'. In Judah, Jeremiah had bought a piece of land at Anathoth when the destruction of Jerusalem was only months away; it was a token that some of his people at any rate would be returning to their country in the not too distant future; and they did. In Babylon, Jehoiachin did emerge from prison, and descendants of Judah's royal family did go back to Palestine, though most would sink into obscurity until one night, outside another village not far from Jerusalem, shepherds guarding their flocks would hear the unexpected news that 'to them in David's town was born of David's line' a Saviour, Christ the Lord, who was to be the greatest of all the kings. In fact this would be the Invisible King himself made visible for one short human lifetime. Even Egypt was drawn back into the drama: as it was the land of Israel's exile in the time of Moses, and again for some in the time of Jeremiah, so the pattern was repeated in the childhood of Jesus, and Matthew's gospel repeats the words of Hosea's prophecy: 'Out of Egypt I called my son.'

Meanwhile, what exactly was the kingdom, and what would become of it? We have thought of Yahweh as the Invisible King; in what sense might his kingdom also be called 'invisible'?

If in the late 580s you had visited Mount Zion looking for David's throne and Solomon's temple and Jerusalem the city of God, you would have seen none of these things – only a desolate wasteland. But you might have recalled that in the days of the exodus, long before Israel had reached the place where one day a king would reign over it, it was not a place but a people that had been declared by Yahweh to be a 'kingdom of priests'; and from that time forward a kingdom they would always remain, whether or not they had a country, with a visible king on a visible throne.

Then again, when (being now in exile) it was not the ruins of Jerusalem but the oppressive splendours of Babylon that they saw before their eyes, not only were they still Yahweh's kingdom, but they were given to understand that the 'kingdoms of this world' also were under his control. Israel and Judah were already defunct as nation-states when Daniel the prophet stood in the court of Nebuchadnezzar, the master of an empire, and told him to his face that it is the God of Israel who rules all the kingdoms of men, and places over them whom he will.

Moreover, there was never a time when this was not the case. You could go back in biblical history all the way to Genesis 6 and the days of Noah, long before Israel as such even existed, whether as Moses' nation or as Abraham's family, and there you would find (in the words of Psalm 29:10) Yahweh sitting enthroned as King even at the time of the flood, and as King for ever: all the world, through all ages, is his kingdom.

It is an invisible kingdom in the sense that if you are looking for a flesh-and-blood monarch surrounded by the trappings of an earthly monarchy, you can hunt through the greater part of its history and not find them. To the mystified Roman governor's question – 'Are *you* a *king*?' – Jesus replied that his was not the sort of kingdom Pilate had in mind. But for a while, in the days of the kings, the kingdom was visible, embodied in a political nation-state. I have called the Hebrew kingdoms a model, because they represented in miniature what the reign of God is actually like. Often they did it very imperfectly, and sometimes, as in the reigns of Saul and Manasseh and all the northern kings, they did it so badly as to demonstrate by contrast what it is not. But at their best, in a way that no republic, whether totalitarian or democratic, ancient or modern, can match, they show us what life can be like under the rule of an all-wise, all-loving, and all-powerful King.

A NOTE ON THE DATES AND
REIGNS OF THE HEBREW KINGS

If the only things you knew about the Old Testament –
'knew' in inverted commas – were that its contents are
(a) religious, (b) ancient, (c) to judge by the King James
translation insufferably quaint, and (d) mostly either
boring or bloodthirsty, or indeed just plain unbelievable,
then its characters and stories would surely seem the stuff
of myth and legend rather than real history.

The trouble is that over many years now, many people
who actually have studied it have been conditioned to
read it that way, and to discount the real history in it.
They have been told that while its narratives may indeed
be based on facts, by the time they were being written up
the facts had largely been forgotten. Not knowing what life
in David's Israel, for example, was really like, the authors
of Kings and Chronicles pictured it in terms of their own
times, perhaps 600 years later, with one or two unlikely
miracles stirred into the mix to spice it up. Unsurprisingly
therefore we find anachronisms, inventions, distortions,
and errors in their work (so it is claimed), and as history

in the modern sense of the word it is not reliable.

But the truth is that since this idea of the unreliability of the Old Testament took hold, an enormous amount of new information about that ancient world has been unearthed by archaeologists. More and more of the history of the region in the days of the Hebrew kings turns out to have been exactly as the Bible describes it. The 'annals of the kings of Israel' are first mentioned in 1 Kings 14:19, and frequently from then on; and strictly speaking the word is not even 'annals', year-books, but 'journals', day-books, prosaic and factual. These were one source among many, in that nation and other nations of the Middle East, which recorded events *as they happened,* which tally with one another, and which provided the biblical historians with their framework of facts.

The facts include dates. There is no doubt, for instance, that the battle of Qarqar took place in the year we call 853 B.C., and provides an important fixed point in Old Testament history. It too is one of many. Most dates from Solomon onwards are accurate to the year, sometimes to the month and even to the day. Dated events help to steer us away from the notion that the Bible narrative is fiction or romance rather than an account of things that actually happened.

Concerning these dates: in the nature of the case nearly all the events described in this book belong to the centuries 'Before Christ', with just a few references to 'Anno Domini' years. Since it should be obvious which are which, I have put in the letters B.C. and A.D. only sparingly. It would be an insult to the reader's intelligence to remind him or her that we count the B.C. years backwards, but it should perhaps be pointed out that 'the late seventh century' means something like 630–610, and 'the early 630s' are 639–636!

Three other things need to be borne in mind about

the years of the kings, the first being their calendar. In the world of the Old Testament the year began not in the winter, as it does for much of today's world, but in the spring, or indeed sometimes (to confuse things still more) in the autumn. In books more learned than this one, events are often given dates like '749/748', meaning in our terms the year that ran from April 749 to April 748. I have usually given only the second of such pairs of figures, and sacrificed strict accuracy for the sake of easier reading.

Furthermore, there were two different ways of counting the years of a king's reign. Applying them to the modern British monarchy, we should find one system counting the whole of 1952 as the final year of George VI's reign, though he died soon after it began, and none of it as belonging to Elizabeth II's reign. The other system would count 1952 twice, as both his last year and her first year. To put it another way, the first would date her reign from the January following, while the second would date it from the January just past. Every reign is made to seem a year longer by the latter reckoning than it is by the former one. To work out, let alone explain, which of the Hebrew kingdoms used which calendar, and which system of regnal years, at which point in its history, is (thankfully) beyond the scope of this book. There are books that do deal thoroughly with these and similar detailed questions, and some are listed in the final paragraph of this note.

The third thing is related to this matter of the length of a reign. It is easy to miss unless you are reading the text very carefully. If you assumed, as you might, that a king's reign began when his father's ended, so that you could simply add the length of the first to the length of the second and the results would fit in with the rest of the historical data, you would quickly find that they didn't. The method produces insoluble problems, much more complex than the one-year discrepancy that seems to arise from the regnal-year differences.

But again the British monarchy provides an analogy. Elizabeth II acceded to the throne early in 1952, but was not crowned till the summer of 1953. She 'became queen' twice, in two different senses, first at her accession and then at her coronation. This should alert us to the fact that when the Old Testament speaks of the start of a reign, it may not mean what we think it means. In one way or another Solomon 'became king' no fewer than three times (1 Kings 1:35, 1 Chronicles 29:22 and 28). The significant thing in his case, affecting the Hebrew kingdoms generally, is that his reign began before his father's had ended.

As we have noticed frequently, later kings saw how useful the overlap between David and Solomon had been, and extended this system of 'co-regency' greatly, so that a son might be his father's 'associate king' for several years. Uzziah's fifty-two-year reign, for instance, both begins and ends with long co-regencies, and it is only for seventeen years in the middle that he is actually 'sole king'.

Readers eager to explore the subject further should note a number of names. The standard work on Old Testament history has long been John Bright's *A History of Israel* (London 1960/2001), but where the dates and reigns of the Hebrew kings are concerned there are much newer works that need to be consulted alongside it. Edwin Thiele (*The Mysterious Numbers of the Hebrew Kings*, Chicago, 1951; Grand Rapids 1965/1986/2008), Gershon Galil (*The Chronology of the Kings of Israel and Judah*, Leiden, 1996), Kenneth Kitchen (*On the Reliability of the Old Testament*, Grand Rapids/Cambridge, 2003) and Leslie McFall ('The Chronological Data in Kings and Chronicles,' Bibliotheca Sacra, vol 148, 1991, and other works available online, via website www.btinternet.

com/~lmf12) are the authors and titles to look for. To
Professor Kitchen's vast knowledge of biblical archaeology,
I am indebted for many good things, not least the
memorable place-name 'Davidopolis'. To Dr McFall, I
owe my warmest thanks for his personal interest and for a
wealth of closely-reasoned dating.